Warning:

Firearms are potentially dangerous and must be handled responsibly. The information contained in this training program is not meant to be used by a novice, or by someone who has not received proper instruction. The information in this book is intended for academic study only unless the reader complies and ensures that they receive proper instruction on the use of and safety procedures required for firearm use. The author, Shooting-Performance, and any party associated with either assume no liability if injury, death, or unintended damage occurs during the use of this program or from information contained in this book. If you do not wish to comply with safe firearm practices, please return this book for a full refund, and **do not read any further!**

By: Mike Seeklander

Introduction to the Author:

Shortly after buying Shooters Paradise in Woodbridge, VA, I had the urge to put together a competition shooting team. It started out as simply a way to give myself a small tax write off, but I figured I might as well help out a few friends along the way. I still remember having a conversation with one of my best friends, Ron Francisco, nearly 10 years ago. "You need to sponsor Mike Seeklander," he said. "Mike who?" I responded.

Actually, I had met Mike a couple years earlier at the USPSA Limited Nationals, but didn't really remember. Maybe it was because I was too wrapped up in my own rise to the top. Maybe it was because I was too distracted by all of the world-class shooters I was in the mix with...the same people I had read about and idolized for several years. When I stop and think about Mike and his personality, I know now that it was probably because he was unassuming and modest. Just a quiet guy who is now a top-level competitor and instructor, but you would never know it unless you pried it out of him yourself.

I'll never forget our first trip together when we travelled to the 2003 South Carolina Section Championship. I had already established myself as a top contender in practical shooting, and Mike was the most inquisitive person I had ever met. He wanted to know everything from my training regiment, to what I saw when the gun fired, to what I ate before a match! I just assumed back then that he was merely making small talk. Now I realize that whenever I gave him my take on things, he was processing everything I said. He was systematically laying the bricks in the foundation of his future career as a professional shooter and instructor...whether we knew it or not!

Throughout the years, our jobs have changed, as well as our professional relationship. But I've still managed to see that he is one of the most analytical shooters on the planet. His questions and endless quest for knowledge surely didn't stop with me. He went on to pick the brains of many of the best competitive and tactical operators in the world, morphing his findings with his own techniques and styles into an easily usable and understandable guide to success.

Mike and I still compete and train together today. We share the same love for the sport of competitive shooting, the same drive to succeed, and the same commitment to improving others in the sport; hell...we even share the same birthday! On the other hand, we have reached our goals in very different ways. Mike has managed to pave a very defined and logical path to success...one that I'm confident that anyone who is interested in improving their shooting will benefit from. I only wish he would have written this book 15 years ago!

It is my hope that you will benefit from Mike's hard work as much as he has. I can promise you that the only way to make it happen is to TRAIN HARD!

Phil Strader

President/CEO

Straighter Solutions, LLC

Welcome!

Thank you for purchasing this training program/book. It is best used in conjunction with the logbook that accompanies it, "Your Performance Logbook". This training program will take you to the next level in your skill development. I hope that it helps you accomplish your shooting goals, and teaches you how to train.

If you are like me, you were not graced with superstar natural talent, and have to work for every ounce of skill you have. If so, then this logical program will guide you through a routine that will ensure your success. Once you are done with the program, you will be able to self-critique yourself and continue to improve your skills by modifying the program and drills to meet your needs. Lastly, I want to admit that I am a shooter and professional instructor, not a writer. That being said, this book has been through an extensive editing process, but some of you with a keen eye may catch areas that are written in a manner less formal, which is my intent. I wanted to speak to you as shooters, in plain English! (For the really keen, if you catch a spelling error, please let me know)

Special thanks go to several people who have specifically helped me with this book and the training program that accompanies it:

➢ Rich Brown – editing, style, and grammar.

➢ J. T. - edited the training drills.

➢ Jeff Rosenlund – for editing, and grammar for another version of this book, most of which is contained within.

➢ John Hill - editing, ideas, and reality checks.

➢ Tim Egan - detailed drill schematics (he did the coolest stage diagrams in a major match booklet [Area 1] that I have ever seen).

To order your copy (if this isn't) of "Your Competition Handgun Training Program" or "Your Performance Logbook", please visit my website: www.shooting-performance.com

By: Mike Seeklander

Mike Seeklander Biography

I am known as a nationally ranked competitor on the practical handgun competition circuit. Most people fail to realize that I have extensive formal training and experience in

the military and law enforcement as an operational police officer, U.S. Marine, Federal Air Marshal, and Federal firearms instructor. I also have formal training in delivering instruction as well as in all phases of training development. I began my competitive shooting training to increase my skill level for a future fight with a handgun or rifle. After getting my feet wet at a few competitions, I found myself motivated to reach the elite levels of practical shooting. During this time I realized the importance of using efficient and correctly designed training programs to help reach my goals.

I am the recipient of numerous awards and honors in the law enforcement community, and on the competitive shooting circuit. While working full time, in various occupations, I have placed highly in every major practical type championship on the circuit. I have numerous wins at major matches including a second place finish at the 2007 European Handgun Championship, and top five finishes at the U.S. Nationals, the World Speed Shooting championships and NRA Action Pistol championships. I am classified as a Grandmaster (multiple divisions) by the United States Practical Shooting Association and a Master by the International Defensive Pistol Association. As the Director of Training at the U.S. Shooting Academy, my primary focus is instructor training, curriculum development, and specialized instruction. I have developed lesson plans, curriculum, and specialize in teaching the following:

- Intermediate and Advanced Competitive Handgun Shooting Techniques
- One Handed Survival Shooting Techniques
- Vehicle Tactics
- Close Quarters/ Extreme Close Quarters Shooting Techniques
- High Performance Handgun Techniques (combative application of competitive technique)
- High Performance Rifle Techniques (translating the performance side of competitive shooting to the combative arena)

Shooting-Performance, my consulting/training company-

- I began Shooting-Performance (www.shooting-performance.com) as a free information sight where I could share my thoughts and lessons learned with the shooting community. That evolved into consulting, coaching, and some published material such as this book, and a couple others (that are being finalized as I write this), as well as numerous magazine and forum articles. My original interest and passion lay not in teaching specific technique (as I believe it should always evolve), but in getting shooters from all walks of life to understand how to make their training more effective. Most of my students ask a common question after they have a good grasp on how to perform the techniques taught in a class, and that is: How should I train? Answering that question has been my passion ever since. Promoting the concept of correct design and perfect execution of training programs (and drills) was my primary motivator in developing Shooting-Performance.
- There is a wealth of useful information in the form of web pages, documents, and some video. You will also find a question form that will allow you to send me a question and get answers. Please visit my website and drop me a line if you have a shooting comment, question, or revelation!

Contents:

CHAPTER ONE
Introduction
to the Program

"Relentlessly pursue your preparation, like your life depended on it"

By: Mike Seeklander

The topics I will cover in this chapter:

1. *Overview of the training program*
2. *Program length*
3. *Training modules in the program*
4. *Technique discussion*
5. *Pieces of the program (yearly plan, training matrix, daily training plan, training drills, log sheets)*
6. *Frequently Asked Questions*
7. *Program Principles (principles of an effective training program)*
8. *Additional program principles*
9. *Monthly Training Matrix*
10. *Yearly plan*

Introduction to the Program

How to use this program- Read this entire program/book before you begin it. Getting an overall feel about how this thing will work is very important. Please take the time to read it and get an idea about how the program will work before you begin.

What it will do for you- Whenever I teach a class, I try to give a clear and concise statement at the start of the class describing what the class will do for the student. I would like to do the same thing for this program. Only you can ultimately guarantee your success with consistent hard work, but this program will give you a clear path to follow on the road to that success. I would expect you to jump one or more classes (the International Defensive Pistol Association and United States Practical Shooting Association classify shooters based on their skill, for more information visit their websites) at least if you complete this program from start to finish, and most of you will reach the upper classes (Master or Grandmaster) of the USPSA or IDPA classifications if you follow it for a year or more. The biggest obstacle to most people reaching their shooting goals is the lack of a definitive plan. This book and the program contained inside it has the work done for you. If you are a shooting athlete in the practical shooting circuit (consisting of IDPA, USPSA, or specialty sports like Steel Challenge and NRA Bianchi) this book will give you a solid training program to follow for the shooting season. It is complete and ready for you to execute now, resulting in your success!

IDPA vs. USPSA skills- This book and the program contained within is equally effective for either sport and will also help you succeed in the specialty sports. When writing this program, I knew that it would be used by athletes that specialized in USPSA, as well as IDPA (and maybe the specialty sports). Therefore, I designed it to work just as efficiently for each sport. The key to success in any sport is performing on demand the techniques required to win. The athletes winning USPSA are the same ones winning IDPA. The commonality is in the shooting. The training drills you will do with this program are designed as dual use drills. You will modify them slightly when you decide to use them for another sport like IDPA, by simply putting on a cover garment or adding a piece of simulated cover to work around. I will expand more on this later.

How long will it take? - I design my programs for an entire season and break down the season into post, pre and during season areas. This allows the athlete to go through cycles where they are focusing on key components that need to be done to succeed, all of which are not necessarily [shooting] training. Preparation is much deeper than just going to the range to practice, and this program will take you through all phases of preparation, including gear selection and preparation. The program is a year in length, as I will address and assign you things to do in your off season. The live fire (in season) training cycle will be sixteen (16) weeks in length. I will also give you some tips on maintaining your skills after you have finished the 16 week cycle. You will complete the program over an entire shooting season, which for almost all shooting sports is from February thru October. I recommend that you set yourself a target date so that you can finalize your 16-week program a month or more before the biggest match you plan to shoot in the season. This will allow you to modify and fine-tune your skills, so that you peak and are at your best during that big match.

Program Overview - The following table will list the elements of the program that you will go through during your training year. Understand that we will also have a modification plan that will allow you to increase or decrease your sessions per week and still get the value you need. The following is the minimum I recommend if you are very serious and want to really increase your skill over a shooting season. The program can/should be repeated over multiple seasons, and one of the last chapters of this book discusses the process of reviewing your season notes and modifying your program. The program consists of three separate phases of training. These three phases will increase in difficulty as you go through the program. Phase II and III will include tougher drills because of the increased distances and more complex drills. All training drills will be simple, yet effective.

An overview of the program (you may modify this slightly under my guidance).

Training Module	Time Invested (per week)
Live Fire. *3 live fire training sessions per week (A, B, and C training session each focusing on a key skill area). The program is also designed to allow you to do more or less depending on your individual circumstances.*	3 hours
Dry Fire. *3-5 dry fire training sessions per week (These 15 minute session will focus on your manipulation skills).*	1 hour
Visual Training. *3 Visual training sessions per week.*	1 hour
Mental Toughness Routine. *Weekly mental toughness routines (Mental training will help you connect better with what you are doing and perform on demand)*	1 hour
Physical Fitness. *3+ physical fitness training sessions per week will be a strong recommendation.*	3 hours
Match. *1 club/local match per month (We need to have a way to assess our skills and see if our program is working. Evaluating your skill by taking small "quizzes" along the way is the key).*	4 hours
Your total time invested (including a match and your fitness routine):	**13 hours**

By: Mike Seeklander

6 modules of success - There are 6 key areas that you will focus on to ensure your success. They are: live and dry fire training, visual training, mental training, physical fitness, and game day quizzes (matches). The symbiotic effect of doing all of these training modules in a systematic manner will increase your skill more than the raw results of them just added together. Your training program will be a systematic set of processes that will give you the skills needed to reach your goal, rather than a random set of practice sessions that are unlikely to work as well. You will make much more progress with this program than just by doing random training drills.

Technique – It is important that you already have some fundamental skill with a firearm before beginning this program. It is designed to increase your skill in applying the fundamentals of technique on demand, in a systematic manner of training. I STRONGLY recommend that if you are new to shooting, you take a class or find an instructor (please contact me for information about training) that can teach you the basics before beginning so you will understand the details behind all of the techniques you need to succeed in your sport. This book was not meant to be a technique book, rather a book where you increase your ability to perform techniques better and better, allowing you to succeed in your performances. I have included a short bonus section on technique at the end of the book, taken from the Shooting-Performance coaching manual, because it offers an explanation of certain terms and concepts I discuss in this book.

I am a believer that technique should evolve constantly, which is one of the reasons I did not want to write a "how to" book about technique. Honestly, if I had, I would probably have made changes in my own technique before it made it to the printing press. You should never stop looking for a better way to do business and that includes finding better techniques or modifying your current system. If however you need instruction on proper technique, here are some recommended sources of proper technique in order of their effectiveness:

> ***Classes***: There are several good instructors out there that can get you up to speed with technique. Obviously I prefer you contact me first, since this is my program. If I am not available, there are several good instructors I can recommend. (Contact me for more information about classes: mikeseeklander@shooting-performance.com) Without correct technique, training drills become irrelevant because you are ingraining the wrong skillsets into your subconscious mind, so get some training if you need it.

> ***Video***: If you can't get to a class in person, you can get a ton of good information from a video. I own most, if not all of the USPSA/IDPA technique related videos that are on the market and I have learned a great deal from them. They will not substitute for a class and the feedback you will get from a professional instructor, but you can learn a great deal from a video. This book will have a DVD that accompanies it if you are more of a visual learner.

13

By: Mike Seeklander

Please visit my website for more information or to order the DVD (expected early 2011 depending on production).

➤ **Books**: Books are another way of exploring various techniques. Like videos, my library contains volumes of shooting related books (I think almost every one that has been written on the subject of training and competitive shooting). I have really learned some great things from them. However, books are last on my recommended sources of technique list because it is hard to learn manual technique from a book.

Key Parts of a Training Program - Your training program is broken down into different pieces, which serve a separate purpose. They are as follows:

> ➤ *Yearly Plan*
> ➤ *Monthly Training Matrix*
> ➤ *Daily Training Plans*
> ➤ *Training Drill Sheets (live and dry fire)*
> ➤ *Log Sheets*

Please see the next page for a chart that shows the relationship of each of these pieces.

The following chart will give you an idea of what each piece of your training program will do for you.

Piece	Purpose
YEARLY PLAN	Your yearly plan will be your guiding force for the entire training year. I strongly recommend laying out your year in some sort of one page view so you can chart out different events and training cycles. In the sports world this is called periodization, which means the training year is divided up into different periods to allow for peaking during the right time.
MONTHLY TRAINING MATRIX	Your Monthly Training Matrix will allow you to overlap all training types (categories) in a given month so you can ensure that you will actually be able to accomplish all of the training you need to do in your program. You will chart out the frequency and duration of each component as well as what days you plan to perform them. This document will help you make sure everything will "fit".
DAILY TRAINING PLAN	Your Daily Training Plan will be your actual daily training plan. You will follow one of three separate plans (Sessions A, B, and C), each containing different drills. Your training plans will vary in each of the three phases.
TRAINING DRILL SHEETS	Your Training Drill Sheets will have all key details for each drill. They are detail oriented in order to keep you consistent in your training.
TRAINING SESSION LOG	Your Training Session Log's are sheets that you will use to log all details of each training session. I pre-design and print mine in order to save time when I am at the range. This keeps me from having to write the headings over and over again. I have a preformatted logbook that you can purchase to use with this program (it has dry fire, live fire, event, and other great log pages for an entire training year). Visit my website for more information.
MATCH or EVENT LOG	Your Match/Event Log's are similar to training logs but are formatted so that they capture key stuff from the event you will be participating in.

15

Frequently Asked Questions - I thought that you would have some questions so I have decided to try and address them before you ask (once you have read this program, I am available for you if you have further questions, simply visit my website and email me or fill out the question form). They are as follows:

1. *"This program is very detailed and specific. Is it necessary for me to follow it exactly?"*

   o *Answer:* I recommend that you follow the program as closely as possible for the first 16 weeks or more. I have done the work for you in this program, so you can focus on training! Small modifications are ok, but give the whole program a chance to succeed before you start modifying it.

2. *"Can I use my own drills or drills from programs like Rob Leatham's drillmaster, etc. with this program?"*

   o *Answer:* Yes, you may supplement the program with other drills as long as you have taken the time to ensure the additional drill is well designed. Do the drills that I have assigned in this program, and then add some additional drills to your training sessions if you choose to do so.

> **Coaches Note:**
>
> "You don't know what you don't know"- This phrase means that if you are new to anything, you may not know what you are missing. For this reason I highly recommend asking before you waste you training time and precious ammunition if you do not understand something. Please visit my website and ask away.

3. *The drills don't seem complex, like a stage would be. Will they teach me what I need to know?*

   o *Answer:* Yes, you might be able to build and do more complicated drills, but all of mine are designed with the minimalist concept in mind. I know most of you have very limited time, equipment, and range limitations that require simple yet effective drills to do the job. With four targets, a few props, and key information I promise to teach you more with my drills than you would learn by setting up and shooting complex stages. I believe you should develop your skills and think of them like pieces of a puzzle. When you have to "put the puzzle together" i.e. shoot a complex stage, simply pick the pieces you need and fit them together.

4. *How do I refer to the drills while at the range?*
   o *Answer: You can certainly take the book with you, but for your convenience if you email me with proof of purchase of this book, I will email you a smaller PDF version of the drills that you can take to the range.*

5. *Is there another reference such as a video of these drills?*
   o *Answer: In a short period of time I will be completing a DVD with the training drills in action. This will greatly assist you in seeing what they look like when performed.*

17

Program principles

Principles of an effective training program - In order for this or any program to be effective, it must follow certain principles. The training program in this book will follow these principles:

- ***Training drills must be designed correctly.*** This is the first validation of your program. It couldn't be more simple, but this is often the area that I see wrong with most programs/drills that I have come across during my career. The learning goals must be thought out and defined and then applied throughout the drills that are used. Even programs developed with the best intent will be problematic if you don't pay attention to design. There are two key things that correctly designed training drills must do:

> **Coaches Note:**
>
> I have painstakingly designed all of the training drills in this program so that they will replicate and produce the skills you will need to perform. Make sure you read them and follow them completely.

  - o Skills developed must be applicable with the key factors desired (environment, gear, dynamics).
  - o Skills developed must replicate the actual key skills needed. (This is an area that some really good athletes/operators argue about because everyone has a slightly different idea about what techniques and tactics will be "needed".)

- ***Training repetitions must be executed perfectly.*** Once training drills are developed so that they produce the two desired results listed above they are designed correctly. This is not enough though, and now the person doing the training (you) must ensure that each repetition is done perfectly in order to ingrain correct skills. If the training repetitions are done wrong, this will build subconscious skill programs that are wrong, and the end user will get the wrong result when they try to perform the skill trained (usually under pressure). This principle is simple, and is a key component to success in your training program.

- *Training sessions must be done at regular intervals*. In order to develop skill (which is the purpose of your training program), the brain and neuromuscular system must be exposed to developmental sessions on a regular basis. How often is debated, and will generally depend on the goal. But across the board almost all of the experts agree that development must take place a minimum of two times every week or more during the initial learning phase, and then one time per week to maintain skill.

- *Training sessions must be documented*. In order to reflect on the program's success or failures, training sessions must be documented. Key metrics should be written down for future reference. You will use this data to modify the program as you go. Measurement is only possible if documentation is done. (See next principle)

- *Skills and abilities developed must be measured*. Simply "feeling" that you are improving is a dead end road. Take the time to measure your skills on a regular basis. Someone once said that something that can be measured could be improved. It's true. Measure your skills regularly to guide you through the program modification phase.

- *Must be modified based on results (game day)*. A good training program *must* be modified. If not, results will stagnate and skills will remain in one place. Therefore, you will need to reflect on your training logs and modify your program to continue your evolution. If you have

By: Mike Seeklander

done the job of logging your metrics and key details, the answers will be there for you do find.

Move fast, shoot in control - This is a principle I teach in all of my classes, and simply put, it means that you should focus your training repetitions on increasing the speed with which you move to get the gun on target. Shoot the shots as fast or slow as needed to get the hits that will make you successful in a match (A's and 0's). Lets say for example, you are working on the draw and firing cycle with a drill that has three targets, each a different distance away (5 yards, 10 yards, and 25 yards). If you performed a draw and fired two shots on each of those targets, in three separate strings, your draw-speed (actual movement to get your hand on the gun, and out of the holster) should be relatively the same to the point when you are stopping the gun on the target and managing the trigger. Each of those targets would take a different level of sight focus and trigger manipulation to hit them correctly, so those speeds would be different, but the movement to draw the gun from the holster to the target should be the same. You can apply this principle to any physical movement you are working in any drill, such as a turn or step, etc. Your *movement* must be fast (as fast as technically possible), and the shooting (when you get the gun on target) must be in control, allowing you to get good hits.

As fast as you can perform them technically correct - I get a question regularly from my students when we are working on drills. They ask if they should be going fast or slow on the drill they are working on. My answer surprises them: "Neither!" You should not focus on going fast or slow, you should focus on performing each technique as fast as you can while still performing it *technically* correct. What does "technically correct" mean? It means that you perform the technique in a manner that allows you to focus on and correctly execute all of the small parts of the technique right. The better you get at the technique, the faster you will be able to perform it technically correct. Theoretically, this is a positive feedback loop of executing training technique repetitions as fast as you can do them, yet still technically correct.

If you miss a session, just make it up later, don't skip it - When we get to the live fire section of this program, I will assign you three different sessions, each focusing on a different skill area. You will rotate through these three sessions weekly (or more or less depending on your personal situation). While I want you to get in three live fire training sessions per week, it's ok to do a bit less if something comes up. However, if you miss a session I want you to make it up the next time you train. Don't skip over it and go on to the next session.

Your Training Schedule - You will be doing different things during different times of the shooting year. I built this program with the normal U.S. season in mind (shoot Feb-Oct, and off Nov-Jan), but you can slightly adjust it if necessary. Just make sure you focus on the areas I am assigning you during the timeframes listed. It is broken down into *Post/Off* Season, *Pre-Season*, and *In-Season* timeframes. As stated before, you will be doing your actual live and dry fire 16-week training program during the *In-Season* timeframe, starting it so that you peak about a month before the most important match you will shoot. The following lists what you will focus on during those timeframes:

Post/off season -

> *Relax and Refresh!* I mandate for myself a month or so away from the gun and shooting matches. Even if I just train with a different weapon for a while, and change some things up, I make myself get away from my primary gun and sport. I recommend the same for you. Your season probably ends about October each year, so November and most of December are your off months. We will accomplish some things during your "off season", but the live fire

21

training slows down or stops and you should focus on re-energizing from a hard season.

➢ *Review (previous seasons notes and video).* The post season is a great time to review what you did during the season. Get your training and event logs together as well as your video, and see if you can summarize the data into a format that will allow you to learn from it and set new goals for the next season. I will cover this in more detail in a later section of this book, because after following this program for a season, you will have some detailed notes and video.

➢ *Gun and Gear Check.* Now is the time to get all of your gear and guns and do a detailed inspection of them. Check for broken pieces or parts and wear and tear that will affect you next season. If you are new to this sport and do not have gear, then you need to be researching and ordering what you need. I will include a short gun and gear selection section at the end of this book for new shooters. When you do your inspection, remember that you might not be shooting/handling the guns much throughout November and December, so get them cleaned (detailed cleaning) and oiled for the winter. This detailed cleaning will reveal possible wear and tear that might cause you to have to replace the gun. If you need a new gun for next season (some guys go through a gun a year), then go ahead and get it ordered, because it is likely that you will need to do some stuff to it like sights, trigger, and grip modification. Ordering it now and getting it set up early will allow you to focus on training during the season versus gun and gear issues.

Pre-season - Pre season for this program is a window not far off from your post-season break. I recommend that you start some of this stuff during your post-season break to get ahead of the curve and ensure you have everything you need to have this done on time. This is probably part of December and January for those shooting IDPA and USPSA.

➤ *Logistics.* Ok, you have taken some time off and are gearing up for the next season. Its time to look at your yearly plan and order the supplies you need. This includes:

  o *Ammunition or loading components*

  o *Replacement gear or upgraded parts/components (if you are switching gear for the new season)*

  o *Support Equipment (Pro grip, grip tape, pasters, targets, etc.)*

  o *Books and Videos (if this is a source you plan to get technique from).* *Note:* **Spend your money on knowledge versus trick gear. Knowledge and skill will win over trick gear and fancy guns every time.**

➤ *Physical Training Program (more in chapter six).* The pre-season is the perfect time to start a hard-core fitness program. Therefore, this is when I will place it in your yearly plan. If you are new to this type of training, then I highly recommend you begin it early in the pre-season so you can get used to a regular physical training regimen as well as build a strong base of fitness.

➤ *Set Goals (will be covered in detail in the next chapter).* You will set your goals in the pre-season. This will help you pick the support gear and supplies you will need for the season. The loftier the goals, the more you will have to put into it. I will go into more detail in the next section where you will actually write down your goals.

➤ *Visual Training Program (covered in chapter seven).* The visual training program is best done in the pre-season and then maintained during the season with the exercises done less frequently, and the visual stimulus that your dry and live fire sessions will give you.

By: Mike Seeklander

In-season - During the season you will be hitting all of your training modules hard and heavy. The training matrix will help you get an overall view of how all of these pieces of the puzzle will fit together.

> ➢ *Training Modules (live, dry, mental, physical, visual).* I believe in a systematic method of training and I always try to train the whole spectrum instead of just focusing on one area. I believe this will cause a synergistic effect on your results, which means that you will get more out of the sum of all pieces put together because they compliment each other.

> ➢ *Document and Modify.* You will be documenting everything you do, so you can modify your program as necessary. I would prefer you begin modification of it after you have gone through your 16-week cycle at least once, and have gained the knowledge to do so.

Monthly training Matrix - This is an overall picture of your training modules, and their frequency and duration. The days that you do the sessions can be varied, but the frequency and duration of each training module should be followed as closely as possible.

Training Type	Frequency (How often)	Days/Times (When)	Purpose/Notes:
Live Fire Practice (may also be supplemented with .22 practice)	3 times weekly	**Your choice**	Three separate sessions, each focusing on a certain area.
Dry Fire Practice (may be supplemented with air soft practice)	3-5 times weekly	**Your choice**	Where the real development occurs.
Mental Training (must be integrated in all live and dry sessions!)	5 times weekly	**Your choice**	Performance, Self Image boosting statements, Active and Passive visualization
Physical Training	3-6 times weekly	**Your choice**	Begin Jan 1
Visual Training	3 times weekly	**Your choice**	7 exercise program
Game Day Application (this will be a club or major match)	1 time monthly (minimum)	**Your choice**	All matches should be treated the same.

By: Mike Seeklander

Yearly Plan – The following is a sample yearly plan, which you can look over to see what the entire shooting year looks like. In the logbook that goes with this program *"Your Performance Logbook"*, there is a blank yearly plan for you to fill out.

2010 Competitive Season				
Dates and events		**Key Dates Training Program Modules**		
Month	*Major Events/dates*	<u>Live Fire</u>	<u>Dry Fire</u>	<u>Physical Fitness</u>
January	Base fitness, general skills	01/02	01/02	Begin 12-week fitness program 01/02. Begin dry fire skill program 01/02.
February	USPSA skills Florida Open		02/18	Begin 12-week USPSA skills program 02/01.
March	USPSA skills			End 12-week fitness program, maintenance program. Begin 12-week USPSA program 03/01
April	USPSA skills	Single Stack Nationals	04/02	
May	Bianchi skills (NRA Action)	Bianchi Cup	05/15	
June				
July	Steel Challenge skills			Begin Steel challenge program
August	Steel Challenge skills	Steel Challenge	08/23	
September				Begin USPSA skills program 09/01
October				
November				End Season Review

Summary: Lets summarize the Program:

☐ This program is a complete training program that is 16 weeks in length, which is designed to increase your skill dramatically in the practical shooting sports. Key concepts of the program are:
  o USPSA vs. IDPA skills- the program is designed to be flexible for either sport, and has a section that also covers specialty sports.
  o Length- the program is a year in length, but not all of that year is taken up by actual firearm training. I approach each training year with different components that will occur at specific times.

☐ There are 6 modules of success in the program:
  o Live fire training
  o Dry fire training
  o Mental toughness routine
  o Physical fitness
  o Visual training
  o Match/Events

☐ The program is not designed to teach technique and more information about proper technique can be found on my DVD (in early 2011), or at a class taught in your area. For more information about this, please visit www.shooting-performance.com

☐ There are several pieces of the program:
  o The *Yearly Plan*, which is designed to allow you to plan your entire shooting year.
  o The *Monthly Training Matrix*, which will allow you to plan your training month, and plug all modules into it.
  o The *Daily Training Plans*, which are the actual training plans that will be followed on each training day.
  o The *Training Drills*, both live fire and dry fire drills that will facilitate the development of your skills.
  o *Log Sheets*, for dry fire, live fire, and events (matches) will allow you to log your performance metrics. (these sheets are also packaged into one logbook that you can order and use, called "Your Performance Logbook", for more information visit my website www.shooting-performance.com)

☐ There are several principles of the training program.
  o Training sessions must be designed correctly.
  o Training repetitions must be executed perfectly.
  o Training sessions must be at regular intervals.
  o Training sessions must be documented.
  o Skills and abilities developed must be measured.

By: Mike Seeklander

- Training must be modified based on results (match or game day results).
- ☐ Some other key concepts.
  - Correct then fast (All techniques will be trained correctly, until speed comes from efficiency).
  - Move fast, shoot in control (movement should be executed as quickly as possible, the shooting at a speed that guarantees hits).
  - Perform drills as fast as you can, while still technically correct.
  - If a session is missed, don't skip it but instead make it up the next time you train.

CHAPTER TWO
Setting Your Goals

"Plan for and create your own success"

By: Mike Seeklander

The topics I will cover in this chapter:

1. *Goal setting overview.*
2. *End Goals.*
3. *Performance Goals.*
4. *Enabling Goals.*
5. *Writing your goals.*
6. *Goal limitations.*
7. *Regular goal review.*

<u>**Setting your goals**</u> - Goal setting is not optional in this program. There is a huge amount of information and research out there that proves that written goals are a big piece of most successful routines. Goal setting my way is the first step in a good planning process for you to follow to get what you want. After you are done writing your goals, you will have done a big part the planning needed to meet your goal. In this program, I have built the training modules so that they are modifiable based on your goals.

<u>**Goal Types**</u> - I break goals into three areas: *End* goals, *Performance* goals and *Enabling* goals. The following definitions of my specific goal types should be easy to understand and follow. I will give you my examples afterward so you can just copy mine if you want (personalize them to your needs though). Definitions and explanations of the three types of goals are:

> ➢ ***End goals***- End goals are the ultimate end state you wish to reach or accomplish. If you could have everything you want (relating to the area we are discussing), what would that be? What is the ultimate end state, if you do everything perfectly and all goes as planned? This program is a year in length, so write your end goal based on the first year you use this program. If you have a loftier end goal, go ahead and write that down, too. Set them

yearly at a minimum. Try to write your end goals so that they are realistic. I don't recommend stating you are going to "win" an event as an end goal in itself, but as a part of an end goal. For example, I like to write my end goals so that I have control over every aspect of the goal. I then write what meeting my goal will allow me to do. Also, make sure you have a timeframe set and include that in your goal, even if it is a broad timeframe. You don't have to list the exact date you will meet your goal unless you actually have that date. I add one more thing to my end goal statement and it is a WIFM (What's In It For Me) line. This is a statement that captures how I believe I will be rewarded for meeting my goal. You can list anything that will motivate you to meet your goal. This statement is very much personal and everyone is motivated by something different, so don't hesitate to be very specific and even selfish here. After all you are the one doing the work. Here are a couple end goal examples:

Version 1 End Goal (Not recommended) - "I will win the 2012 National and World Championships."

Version 2 End Goal (Good) - "During the 2010 and 2011 shooting seasons, I will put in the work and meet or exceed all of my enabling and performance goals, allowing me to be the best practical shooter in the world. This will allow me to win the 2012 World Championships and numerous other matches." WIFM (What's In It For Me): "Meeting this goal will reward me with the realization of meeting my life long goal, one set many years ago. I will reward myself with a vacation to Italy with my wife."

Can you see the difference between version 1 and 2? I might not win a certain match or event if someone shows up that puts in the same amount or

By: Mike Seeklander

more work, and has more natural talent than I do. The truth is that I might get beat. I like to be honest with myself and accept that I am not perfect, and focus on what I can completely control (through my preparation and training) rather than what I cannot. I can't control who is going to show up and what kind of preparation they have done. I can only control what I do. One thing I know is that if I do my preparation like I have planned, then I will have a very good chance at actually winning whatever event I am training for.

➢ **Performance goals** - Performance goals are the performance related goals you must reach in order to meet your end goal. If possible, these should be metric goals that are measurable and thus improvable (numbers). These are the things that you will have to be able to do to actually accomplish your end goals. For example, if you want to win a World Speed Shooting (Steel Challenge) title, you can look at the results from previous years and break them down into measurable performance related goals (skills) that you must be able to do, in order to win that match. You will set performance goals for each major end goal you intend to meet, so if you set your end goals by stating that you will win some key event, you might have different performance goals for each separate event. As you meet your end goal, or as your skill increases, keep raising the bar. Remember, your performance goals are goals that will directly facilitate reaching your end goal.

➢ **Enabling goals** - Enabling goals are the small things that you will have to do to build the skills that will allow you to reach your performance goals, thus allowing you success at reaching your end goal. Enabling goals will be directly related to your training modules. Your enabling goals are already pre-established in this program, but you need to understand what they are and how to write them for future goals you set down the road. In reference to enabling goals (in essence the work that you will need to do), there is one author[1] that has a term that he calls MP100+20, which motivates the athletes he works with to meet their regular training sessions and then strive to do 20% more work than they have scheduled.   What a great motivator! Just remember, your competitor is doing the work....

Writing Your Goals - Okay, now lets get your goals down on paper. Get a piece of paper. Better yet, get onto your computer if you have one and open up a word processing program so you can type your goals and print them. This will allow you to have multiple copies and include one in your training logbook. When you have the piece of paper or computer cranked up, answer the following to the best of your ability:

1. What do you really want to accomplish this season? 2. What is the best result you can imagine? 3. When do you want to accomplish this/them? 4. If there are multiple tasks you see yourself accomplishing if everything goes perfect, what are they? 5. What is in it for you?	*End Goals*
1. What must you be able to perform in order to meet your end goal? 2. What are the performance related metrics that you think will allow you to reach your end goals? (List as many as you can think of)	*Performance Goals*
1. What must you do to accomplish all of these performance goals that you listed? (Be detailed and specific here, this is where most of your real planning will take place)	*Enabling Goals*

---

[1] Jason Selk, 10-Minute Toughness (New York: McGraw-Hill, 2004).

Now that you have some end goal raw material, lets take that information and write it in first person, future tense. I normally start with "I will…" because it is more of an enabler if you write something as if it is a concrete statement that you will follow. Then write your end goal statement (it might have pieces of your performance and enabling goals in it), your performance goals, and your enabling goals. Remember that the focus of this book is the training program I have designed for you, so don't stress this exercise, but do it! Once again, I remind you that many researchers and authors[23] of some of the most cutting edge mental material out there have conclusively proven that you increase your chances of success by writing your goals down, so this is my first assignment for you.

Here is an example for you to review before you start:

End Goal: "I will meet or exceed all of my scheduled training modules and become the best practical shooter in the United States and the world in 2014. This will allow me to win numerous championships including the U.S. National Championships and the World Championship. WIFM (What's In It For Me): "Meeting this goal will reward me with the realization of meeting my life long goal, one set many years ago. I will reward myself with a vacation to Italy with my wife."

Performance Goals: "In order to meet my end goal, I must be able to accomplish the following performance related goals:

➢ A high level of Mental Toughness
➢ Good physical fitness

----

[2] Jason Selk, <u>10-Minute Toughness</u> (New York: McGraw-Hill, 2004).

[3] Gary Mack, <u>Mind Gym</u> (New York: McGraw-Hill, 2001).

- ➢ Two or less penalties at all matches
- ➢ 90% accuracy hit ratio at major matches
- ➢ Speed consistent of 95% of the stage winners on each stage at major matches
- ➢ Marksmanship and Manipulation skills consistent with the top GM's

These performance goals will allow me to perform at the level I need to in order to meet my end goal/s."

Enabling Goals: "I will schedule and execute all of my training sessions, including mental, physical, live and dry fire, visual, and practice matches. I will focus on actively visualizing during all live and dry fire sessions and I will perform passive-visualization utilizing my previous good performances as an 'internal video'. I will prepare better than my competitors, and I will follow my yearly plan and go through all of the preparation steps in order to reach the success level that I desire. I will meet my performance goals specifically by doing the following: (I break my enabling goals down in a chart format, and list each performance goal, and then the corresponding enabling goal below it. Sometimes I list another column to the right of the enabling goal that captures any obstacles that I might have to overcome in reference to that specific enabling goal).

See the next page for my enabling goal breakdown-

35

By: Mike Seeklander

A high level of mental toughness.
➢ Regularly use breathing techniques to improve my performance under stress.
➢ Write and use a *Performance Statement* to control my thoughts.
➢ Write and use a *Self-Image Booster* statement to improve my confidence.
➢ Use passive visualization each time I read my self-image booster and in the mornings and evenings two weeks prior to an event.
➢ Use active visualization regularly, in all training sessions and during all matches.

Good Physical Fitness.
➢ I will exercise 5 times weekly.
➢ I will eat 6 healthy meals per day, each small and nutritious.

Two or less penalties at all matches.
➢ I will plan and visualize on all stages.
➢ I will use my success statement to keep my mind on positive thoughts at all matches.

90% accuracy hit ratio at major matches.
➢ I will perform my training drills with 95% or more accuracy during all training sessions.
➢ I will use my success statement and visual cues to keep my mind on positive thoughts at all matches.

Speed consistent of 95% of the stage winners on each stage at major matches.
➢ I will plan and visualize on all stages.
➢ I will push to my level of control on all stages.
➢ I will use my success statement to keep my mind on positive thoughts at all matches.

Marksmanship and Manipulation skills consistent with the top Grand Masters
➢ I will go through all planned dry fire training sessions weekly, paying attention to detail.
➢ I will execute all planned live fire training sessions weekly, focusing on performing perfectly.
➢ I will track my performance metrics and log the results.
➢ I will analyze and adjust my training sessions in accordance with my results.

Now go ahead and write your own. Don't hesitate to write more than one end goal (I recommend an end goal for every major accomplishment you wish to meet), and be very specific when you write your performance goals and enabling goals.

Limitations - The last step in your goal writing process is to look at your enabling goals and see if there is anything that will limit you or keep you from doing each of those things. Limitations might be time factors, supplies, etc., but you will want to indentify them early. Once you have listed your limiting factors, simply find a way to overcome them. Simply list the limitation and next to it write how you are going to overcome it. What happens if you have a limitation that you can't seem to find a way around? Ask for help! That should be your first step in this program, so reach out there to someone you know that might have a solution for you. Call or email me if you need to, but stay focused on relentlessly finding solutions. If you stay focused on finding the solution this will keep you in a positive state of mind. Last but not least, I want you to understand that there is a possibility that you will realize that you might have bitten off more than you can chew when you were setting your goal. If necessary, modify the goal, or even the timeframe that you set to meet it.

Regular Goal Review - One of my mistakes in the past has been writing good goals and then failing to review them until one day I run across them and realize I did a great job of goal setting and planning my future successes. In truth, I didn't really forget about them, but the intimate details of the goal (mainly the enabling part) often became lost in the activities of daily life. I strongly recommend that (after you write your goals) you conduct regular reviews of them. Read them weekly at a minimum. This can be done in conjunction with your training session, or maybe at a different time of the day, but either way, make sure you do it. Read them in detail and make sure you are meeting the required actionable steps that will make them come true. Your end goal should be a powerful statement written in first person,

By: Mike Seeklander

that will boost your self-image, if read weekly or more. You will increase your accountability to the work that needs to be done to meet your goals, if you review them regularly. It will also give you a high level of confidence when you assure yourself you are on track to meet your end goal. If necessary, you can also modify them slightly if you want. The truth is that our lives are often changing and you might realize that you set your goals to high, or too low. Maybe you picked a timeframe that is unrealistic. If you modify your goals just because the going gets tough, then the goal wasn't really a goal in the first place, it was an unrealistic dream. Modify them for logical reasons that will help you refine them to the point they will help push you to higher levels.

Summary: Lets summarize the Setting Your Goals:

- ☐ Goal setting will be a critical aspect of realizing your desires, and will be a big portion of the planning process needed to ensure your success.
- ☐ There are three types of goals, all interrelated that you will need to write, they are:
  - ○ End Goals- This is the end state you wish to reach.
  - ○ Performance Goals- These are the performance factors that will allow you to reach your end goal.
  - ○ Enabling Goals- These are the things you will have to do in order to develop the ability to perform at your performance goal level.
- ☐ Writing your goals is critical to your success, and if they are not written down, you will not realize the benefit of that process. They should be written in first person future tense.
- ☐ Goals should be reviewed regularly in order to stay connected with them and ensure you remind yourself of where you want to go.
- ☐ Goal setting might take research, and some time to complete, especially in regards to performance and enabling goals since they require certain measurable components (performance metrics).

By: Mike Seeklander

CHAPTER THREE
Dry Fire
Training Module

"Develop the real skills without a single round fired"

By: Mike Seeklander

The things I will cover in this chapter:

1. *Skills trained in the dry fire program*
2. *Safety*
3. *Definitions*
4. *Time and location*
5. *Gear and equipment needed*
6. *Dry fire sessions A, B, and C*

Dry Fire Module

<u>**Purpose of Dry Fire**</u> – Dry fire training will be a huge part of this program. I am absolutely convinced that dry fire will be one of the best training tools I can give you to increase your skill in a short amount of time. It is free, can be done almost anywhere, and will help you develop or improve 90% of the skills you will need to succeed in the game. You will train almost all of your manipulation skills exclusively in these dry fire sessions. We will work on the firing cycle (trigger, sight, and recoil management) in live fire. There really isn't a reason to waste live fire time and ammunition on learning how to do things like draw and reload when you can practice them for free in the comfort of your home. The core development of your skill will be done in this dry fire module.

Coaches Tip:

I know of at least one top shooter that keeps his skill level up (he is a world champion) with dry fire almost exclusively. I maintain most of my own skill with dry fire too, and have found that one commonality in the great shooters I have trained with. Dry fire will be one of the BIG keys to your success, pay attention to this chapter.

Details (how to go through it) -

Safety: This is number one on the list because it is the most important. Follow these rules, or don't dry fire!

➢ Separate yourself from live firearms and ammunition (use a separate room if possible).

➢ Set up small dry fire targets with a backstop that is bulletproof, if at all possible (an extra layer of safety).

➢ Go through a process of thoroughly inspecting all firearms and magazines, as well as your own pockets, for any live ammunition before beginning.

➢ If you use dummy (non-live) training cartridges to simulate the weight in your magazines, make sure they are drilled with holes or painted bright orange or another color that will allow you to identify them as dummy rounds. I recommend having one separate magazine (or two) just for dry fire purposes, so you can keep your dummy ammunition in it.

➢ When you are dry firing, and you have to leave the area for whatever reason, re-inspect yourself for live ammunition when you return.

➢ When you are done dry firing, and return to an area where you may have live ammunition and firearms, do not even think about doing one more repetition… that is how accidents happen.

➢ Follow all standard safety rules when dry firing:

➢ *All guns are treated as loaded.*

➢ *Keep your finger off the trigger until you are ready to shoot.*

➢ *Never let your muzzle cover anything you are not willing to destroy.*

➢ *Be sure of your target, backstop, and beyond.*

By: Mike Seeklander

Definitions - Following are some definitions that will be used in the dry fire module.

> *Technically Correct* - The act of ensuring that all elements of the technique are correct in every possible way.
> *Technical Training Speed (TTS)* - The speed at which you should train when learning a technique. There is no emphasis on going fast here, just performing perfect repetitions.
> *Maximum Technical Training Speed (MTTS)* - The fastest speed you can do any given technique meeting all of the elements of technical correctness.

Time and Location - The best time to go through your dry-fire routine will be up to you. I recommend that you do it during a time when you are fully mentally engaged and have time to focus. Your dry fire sessions should be done during a completely separate time than your live fire sessions. Find a location that meets the safety requirements, and will allow you to move aggressively. If possible, it is best to train on a surface that mimics what you will compete on, although this is tough to do. Be careful that you are not on a surface that will be slippery or cause you problems when you are stepping and pivoting.

Gear - Dress, wear, and use exactly what you would wear in a match. I have seen lots of people just wrap a belt around their t-shirt and dry fire like that, and that does not work well. You should wear the same cloths, shoes, and holster/magazine pouch setup that you will wear when competing. If you wear a Velcro inner/outer belt, wear both during your dry fire sessions. Wear your shooting shoes. Do everything as closely as possible to what you will do in a match.

Equipment needed:

> - *PACT Timer-* You will *need* a PACT or similar timer to do the dry fire module. This is not optional. A timer is such a valuable training tool that you will not be able to do this program without one. Even if you have to skip a couple practice sessions and save the money you would have spent on live ammunition to buy one, please do so. Get a timer that has a loud beep and an easy PAR time function. PAR time is the ability to enter a time and have your timer deliver two beeps, a start beep and a stop beep at the end of the time entered. Having this function allows you to train your skills and begin to lower the time incrementally.
> - *1/3 scale IPSC targets-* I am not sure where I got the ones I use, but they are about 1/3 the size of a regular IPSC target. They are invaluable for dry firing in reduced distance settings (where you have little room space).
> - *Your Gear-* Practice with the exact same gear/clothing that you will compete in, including your shoes if you wear specific ones at matches.

Active Visualization - Integrate active visualization with your sets and repetitions. Each time you do a repetition (one draw for example); see yourself doing it before you do it. "See yourself do it, then do it". This will tie your mental and physical execution together. You can read more about active visualization in the mental section.

A key thought – I hesitated to put this in the book, but think it is a unique training method (dry fire), that has some serious voodoo like potential, so pay attention. Some time ago I was practicing for the Steel Challenge (World Speed

By: Mike Seeklander

Shooting Championships), and had been shooting enough over several days that a tendon had began to hurt in my shooting hand wrist. This tendonitis had been bothering me for the season, and I knew that if I kept shooting the stages over and over that I would risk inflaming it even more. Rather than stopping the practice day (we normally shoot a bunch of practice at the practice range to get grooved in for the match), and giving up, I switched to shooting the stages dry fire only. The learning experience was amazing, and I began to see errors that I had never noticed while shooting live fire. It was such a revelation that I began using this "dry fire" training method on some of my live fire drills (actually on the range, not just in normal dry fire sessions) periodically and found it to be an exceptional way to train, especially when limitations keep from using live ammunition (Now those of you with limited ammunition have no excuse!). Try it some time and you just practice all of your live fire drills in a particular session without shooting live. You will see and learn some things that you have never seen before. A progression from this type of practice would be to do a complete practice session *in only your mind*...imagine the learning possibilities there, you could visualize shooting and never ever fire a bad shot, and could rehearse shooting as good as you can imagine (no pun intended). By the way, yes I have tried this *mental only method* too (during an injury), and have found it to be extremely rewarding. Some of you might ignore this tip, but those that don't will find a new level of mental connection.

Sessions - You will do one of three different sessions each time you dry fire. This will allow you to focus on one skillset and keep your dry fire session short, interesting, and high quality. The sessions will be:

> ➢ Session A- Drawing Skills (Monday, Wednesday)
> ➢ Session B- Reloading Skills (Tuesday, Thursday)
> ➢ Session C- Specialty Skills (Friday)

Sets and Repetitions - You will conduct all dry fire training sessions pretty much the same way. Each skill you work on will be trained with 3 sets of 10+ repetitions. If you desire to do more, that is fine as long as you maintain a high level of quality and attention the entire session. Be very careful not to over train and do repetitions without doing them completely correct. Your sets and repetitions will be broken down as follows for each skill trained:

> *First Set/10 repetitions*- Done at your TTS (technical training speed), which does not have a time. Your emphasis will be ingraining the key details of the technique into your subconscious memory. You will do 10+ repetitions at this speed then move on to your second set when you have done 10+perfect repetitions. This means that you will not count a repetition if you mess one up. If you do make a mistake, stop for a second, and figure out why you made the error. Fix the problem then begin again paying attention to what you just fixed.

> *Second Set/10 repetitions*- Done at your MTTS (maximum technical training speed) or 100% of you maximum "correct" speed. You will do these repetitions as fast as you can, correctly. You should have a recorded time from your last session, or if this is your first time, simply guess what time to do the skill in and plug that into your timer. Adjust the timer accordingly until you have found a time that is the maximum correct speed you can do the skill in. Now perform 10 repetitions (hopefully without a mistake).

> *Third Set/10+ repetitions*- Now begin to drop the PAR time by either .05 or .10 increments or less if necessary. When you do this, you will be below (faster) your MTTS, which is faster than you are used to being able to perform the skill. Try to "catch" this time by pushing harder and finding areas where you can improve your technique. Once you "catch"

47

the time and can repeat that five times, drop the timer another .10 or less/more if necessary. Once you get to the point you can no longer catch the time while doing the skill correctly, log the time you caught as your new MTTS. This is the time you will use in your next session. Remember, when doing these maximum speed sets, you must be seeing the sights and performing the skill so you would get hits in the high scoring zone if you were actually shooting. Don't train yourself to miss in dry fire, as this is a possibility if you train incorrectly.

> *Move to the next Skill*- You will now begin the next skill and do your three sets: TTS, MTTS, and Catch the Timer. **Note**: Eventually you will hit a point where you can no longer drop the times when you are trying to catch the timer. We all plateau eventually, and you will do so too. This means that you have ingrained that manipulation skill to the point where you have no room (or very, very little) to improve. The following table will give you an overview of each of the 3 sessions:

Session	Session A (DRAWING SKILLS) [Monday and Wednesday]	Session B (RELOADING SKILLS) [Tuesday and Thursday]	Session C (SPECIALTY SKILLS) [Friday]
Drill's	*ALL SESSIONS WILL BE DONE WITH 3 SETS FOR EACH SKILL, ONE DONE AT THE TTS (TECHNICAL TRAINING SPEED), ONE DONE AT MTTS (MAXIMUM TECHNICAL TRAINING SPEED), AND ONE DONE TRYING TO "CATCH THE TIMER" (DROPPING TIME IN INCREMENTS)*		
	Stationary Draw Hands Relaxed	Stationary Reload	Draw and Transfer
	Stationary Draw Wrists Above Shoulders	Stepping Reload	Reload and Transfer
	Stationary Draw Barricade	Swinging Reload	Target Acquisitions
	Pivoting Draw	Table Reload	Pick up and Load
	Stepping Draw	IDPA Reloads (Note: only trained if IDPA competitor)	Draw to Alternate Position
	Table Draw		
Total Time	30 minutes	30 minutes	30 minutes

DRY FIRE DRILLS

Stationary Draw Hands Relaxed

Type: Drawing	Total Repetitions: 30+ per start position.

Purpose: To build the manipulation skill of drawing the gun from hands relaxed at sides.

Start position: Hands relaxed at sides.

Target type and setup: One small IPSC set at room distance.

Prop setup: N/A

Action/s: Standing stationary and facing the target, on the start signal of the timer, practice drawing and firing one shot (dry) on the target.

Critical Points: From the start positions, both hands must move at the same time. Move hands to the proper index points (chest and behind the gun)! Work on building the grip pressure the same each time, and make sure you feel the prep of the trigger.

Visual Cues: Focal shift from front target center, to front sight.

Mental Cues: Actively visualize the entire drill.

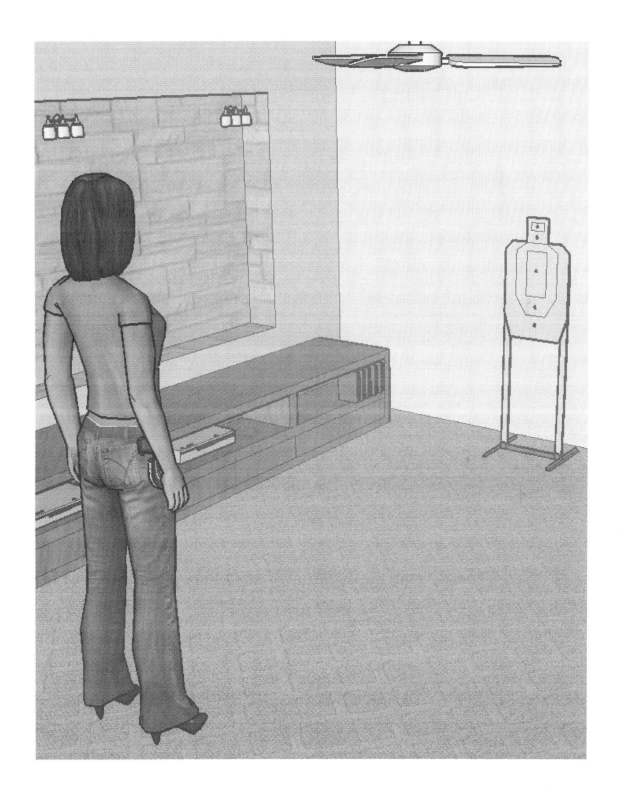

51

By: Mike Seeklander

Stationary Draw Wrists Above Shoulders

Type: Drawing	Total Repetitions: 30+ per start position.

Purpose: To build the manipulation skill of drawing the gun from wrists above shoulders.

Start position: Wrists above shoulders.

Target type and setup: One small IPSC set at room distance.

Prop setup: N/A

Action/s: Standing stationary and facing the target, on the start signal of the timer, practice drawing and firing one shot (dry) on the target.

Critical Points: Both hands must move at the same time, and speed. Move hands to the proper index points (chest and behind the gun)! Work on building the grip pressure the same each time, and make sure you feel the prep of the trigger and verify sight alignment.

Visual Cues: Focal shift from front target center, to front sight.

Mental Cues: Actively visualize the entire drill.

By: Mike Seeklander

Stationary Draw Barricade

Type: Drawing	Total Repetitions: 30+ per start position.

Purpose: To build the manipulation skill of drawing the gun with multiple starting positions.

Start position: Hands on an imaginary (or set up) barricade, about chest height (most match directors will have two X's for hands and they will normally be on the outer edges of the barricade, about chest height).

Target type and setup: One small IPSC set at room distance.

Prop setup: N/A

Action/s: Standing stationary and facing the target, on the start signal of the timer, practice drawing and firing one shot (dry) on the target. You can alternate drawing to the gun side and support side on different training days, but remember that drawing to your gun side is usually the best (and fastest) option.

Critical Points: From the start position, both hands must move at the same time. Move hands to the proper index points (chest and behind the gun)! Work on building the grip pressure the same each time, and make sure you feel the prep of the trigger.

Visual Cues: Focal shift from front target center, to front sight.

Mental Cues: Actively visualize the entire drill.

By: Mike Seeklander

Pivoting Draw	
Type: Drawing	**Total Repetitions: 30+ per start position**

Purpose: To build the manipulation skill of drawing the gun while pivoting.

Start position: Various

Target type and setup: One small IPSC set at room distance.

Prop setup: N/A

Action/s: Imagine yourself in the center of a clock. Begin by standing stationary on a position that would be directly in the center and facing toward the 1 o'clock position. On the start signal of the timer, practice pivoting while drawing and firing one shot (dry) on the target.   After each repetition begin by facing the next number and work your way around the clock. Work an alternate start position and pivoting method for each session, and focus on each of the following start positions and pivoting methods (on Monday work the stepping pivot from the wrists above shoulders, and on Wednesday work the pivoting pivot from hands relaxed at sides). Note: If you don't have an understanding of the difference between stepping and pivoting pivots, see the bonus technique section.

Critical Points: From each of the start positions, both hands must move at the same time. Move hands to the proper index points (chest and behind the gun)! Step forward while pivoting rather than to the rear.

Visual Cues: Head and eyes must snap quickly around to pick up the center of the target before anything else moves. The body will follow.

Mental Cues: Actively visualize the entire drill.

By: Mike Seeklander

Stepping Draw

Type: Drawing	Total Repetitions: 30+ per start position

Purpose: To build the manipulation skill of drawing the gun while stepping.

Start position: Hands relaxed at sides.

Target type and setup: One small IPSC set at room distance.

Prop setup: N/A

Action/s: Imagine yourself in the center of a clock. Begin by standing stationary on a position that would be directly in the center and facing toward the 12 o'clock position. On the start signal of the timer, practice stepping while drawing and firing one shot (dry) on the target while stepping to the 12 o'clock position (you will end standing on the imaginary 12). Re-center yourself and work your way around the clock stepping to each number on the clock. Work your way around the clock by choosing a stepping foot and using that foot until you have gone through all of the numbers.

Repeat with the other foot now. You will be cross-stepping on certain numbers, such as when you are stepping to the left side of the clock (7-11 o'clock) with the right foot.

Critical Points: From the start position, both hands must move at the same time. Start low and stay low, do not stand up when you step into position. When you are stepping, the general rule is that the first foot in must carry most of the weight, and the second foot steps in lightly. Try to end up in the same stance (shoulder width on the balls of your feet) that you started with.

Visual Cues: N/A.

Mental Cues: Actively visualize the entire drill.

By: Mike Seeklander

Table Draw	
Type: Drawing	**Total Repetitions: 30+**

Purpose: To build the manipulation skill of drawing the gun from a table or platform.

Start position: Hands relaxed at sides.

Target type and setup: One small IPSC set at room distance.

Prop setup: A table with a flat surface that is about waste height or slightly below.

Action/s: Begin by standing stationary in front of the table. On the start signal of the timer, practice picking the gun up from the table with a two hand pick up and fire one shot on the target. Modify this drill by picking the gun up and firing on a target to the left or right.

Critical Points: When the timer goes off lower your body to the gun by bending your knees. Pay attention to the trigger finger and ensure it is straight and stays out of the trigger guard!!

Visual Cues: You should start this drill by focusing your vision on the tang (high backstrap) of the gun. The second you grip the gun, shift your vision to the center of the target, and then back to the front sight as the gun gets into position on the target.

Mental Cues: Actively visualize the entire drill.

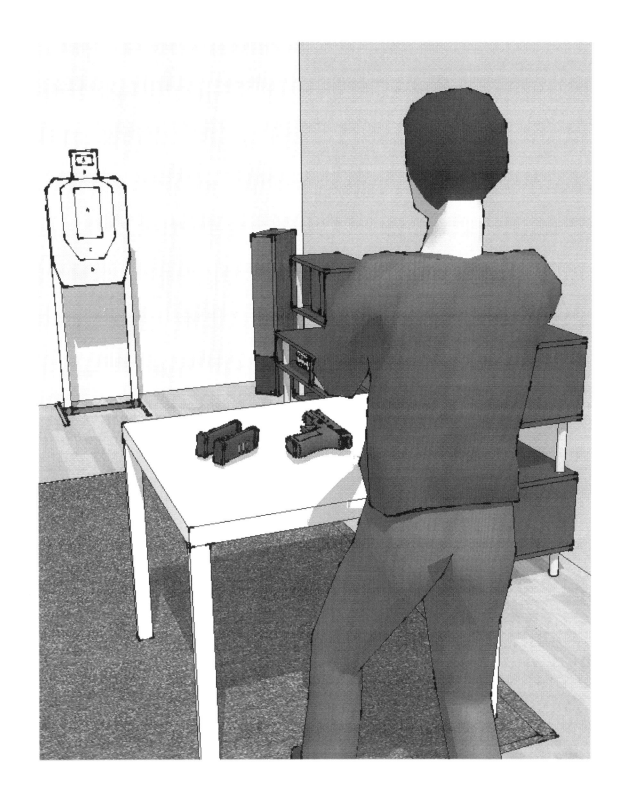

61

Pick Up and Load

Type: Drawing/Loading	Total Repetitions: 30+

Purpose: To build the manipulation skill of drawing the gun from a table and loading it.

Start position: Standing, hands on imaginary marks on the table.

Target type and setup: One small IPSC set at room distance.

Prop setup: A small flat table or similar surface.

Action/s: Begin by placing your hands on imaginary marks. On the timer, pick up and load the gun, and dry fire one shot on the target. You will need dummy rounds for this drill, ENSURE that you use dummy rounds that are specifically marked and easy to identify.

Critical Points: Gun position and magazine position is important. Position them so that they are relatively close to each other. Don't rush this pick up, as this will cause you to fumble the gun or magazine.

Visual Cues: Begin by focusing on the backstrap area of the gun, with the magazine in your periphery. Visual shift back to the target, then the front sight once the gun is on target.

Mental Cues: Actively visualize the entire drill.

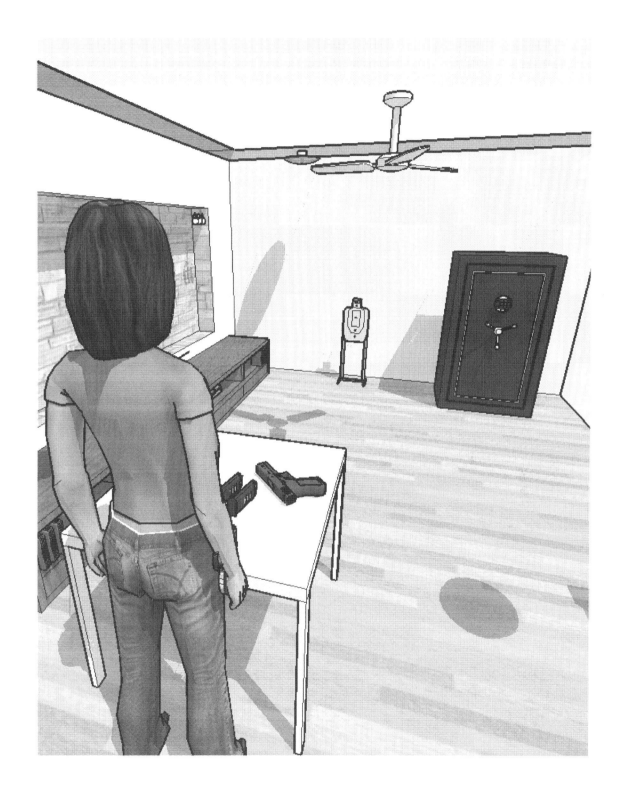

By: Mike Seeklander

Draw to Alternate Position

Type: Drawing	Total Repetitions: 30+ per position

Purpose: To build the manipulation skill of drawing the gun to a squatting, kneeling, and prone position.

Start position: Standing, hands relaxed at sides.

Target type and setup: One small IPSC set at room distance.

Prop setup: N/A.

Action/s: Begin standing centered on the practice target. On the start signal of the timer, practice drawing while moving to position and fire one shot on the target. Practice each position separately (for timing sake). Work the following positions and focus on one (or more if you choose) each training session:

- ➢ Standing to squatting. (Low squat)
- ➢ Standing to kneeling. (Step forward (not backward), or drop straight down)
- ➢ Standing to prone.

Critical Points: Be deliberate when indexing the gun and drawing it from the holster. Make sure to get the gun out before going down into position, so that you don't accidentally point it to the rear, or your legs.

Visual Cues: Begin by focusing on the center of the target. Visual shift back to the front sight once the gun is on target.

Mental Cues: Actively visualize the entire drill.

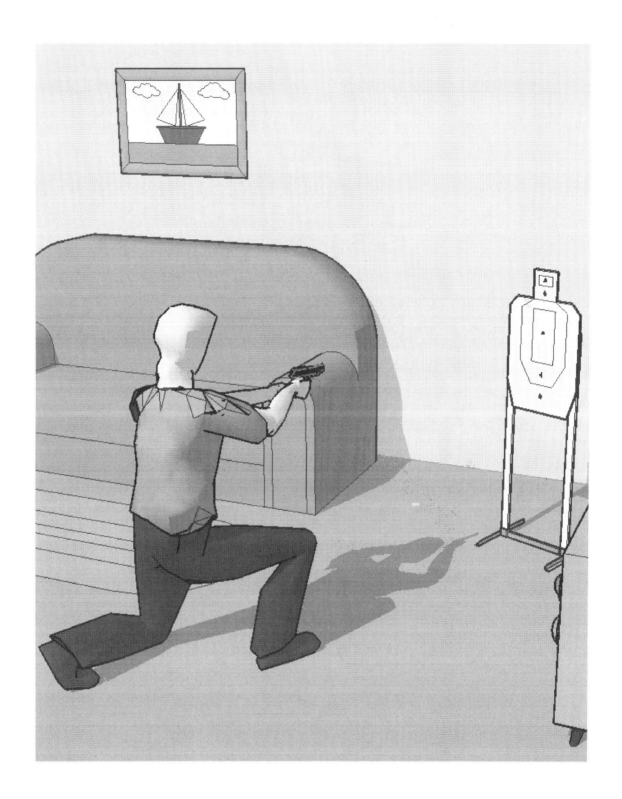

By: Mike Seeklander

Draw and Transfer (support hand)

Type: Drawing	Total Repetitions: 30+

Purpose: To build the manipulation skill of drawing the gun transferring it, and firing with the support (weak) hand.

Start position: Standing, hands relaxed at sides.

Target type and setup: One small IPSC set at room distance.

Prop setup: N/A.

Action/s: Begin standing centered on the practice target. On the start signal of the timer, practice drawing (with the strong hand), transferring the gun to the support hand, and fire one shot on the target.

Critical Points: The gun transfer should happen about midway between the holster and the final extended position. The gun should move in a straight line from the holster to the target. Keep the finger out of the trigger until the transfer and extension of the gun is complete. Ensure that you work on building the grip and prepping the trigger each time.

Visual Cues: Begin by focusing on the center of the target. If necessary, it is ok to look at the tang of the gun while doing the transfer.

Mental Cues: Actively visualize the entire drill.

By: Mike Seeklander

Stationary Reload

Type: Reloading	Total Repetitions: 30+

Purpose: To build the manipulation skill of reloading the gun.

Start position: Gun set up with an empty magazine, hammer/striker cocked, aimed at the target with the finger in the prepped position.

Target type and setup: One small IPSC set at room distance.

Prop setup: N/A.

Action/s: Ensure there is at least one magazine loaded with 1+ dummy rounds to keep yourself from beating the magazine up. (NEVER use live ammunition) On the start signal of the timer, practice reloading, and fire one shot on the target. Practice rotating through and reloading from each magazine pouch (the time should not change) on your belt.

Critical Points: Use the fast/slow/fast concept of getting the new magazine fast, slow down while finding and inserting it into the magazine well, and fast rebuilding your grip and getting the gun back on target. Make sure to index the magazine properly in the magazine pouch.

Visual Cues: Visual shift should go from the front sight, to the magazine well, back to the target center, and finally back to the front sight again during the reload.

Mental Cues: Actively visualize the entire drill.

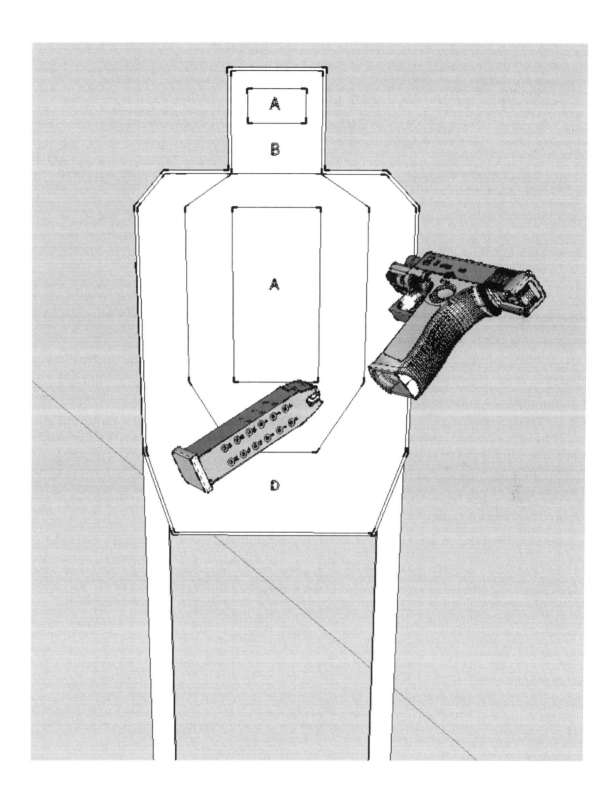

69

Stepping Reload	
Type: Reloading	**Total Repetitions: 30+**

Purpose: To build the manipulation skill of reloading the gun while stepping into another position.

Start position: Gun set up with an empty magazine, hammer/striker cocked, aimed at the target with the finger in the prepped position.

Target type and setup: One small IPSC set at room distance.

Prop setup: N/A.

Action/s: Ensure there is at least one magazine loaded with 1+ dummy rounds to keep yourself from beating the magazine up. (NEVER use live ammunition) Begin in the center of an imaginary clock, facing the 12 o'clock position. On the start signal of the timer, practice reloading while stepping to the 12 o'clock position (you will end up standing on the 12), and fire one shot on the target. Re-center and continue working your way through the clock and stepping to each number. Remember that each step is two foot movements (lead foot steps, and follow foot follows rebuilding the stance in the new position).   Each reload should be finished by the time the second foot hits the ground.

Critical Points: Use the fast/slow/fast concept of getting the new magazine fast, slow down while finding and inserting it into the magazine well, and fast rebuilding your grip and getting the gun back on target. Make sure to index the magazine properly in the magazine pouch.

Visual Cues: Visual shift should go from the front sight, to the magazine well, back to the target center, and finally back to the front sight again during the reload.

Mental Cues: Actively visualize the entire drill.

70

71

Swinging Reload

Type: Reloading	Total Repetitions: 40 +

Purpose: To build the manipulation skill of reloading the gun while moving the gun to another target.

Start position: Gun set up with an empty magazine, hammer/striker cocked, aimed at the target with the finger in the prepped position.

Target type and setup: Three small IPSC set at room distance, one directly in front of the shooter, and one at the 3 and 9 o'clock positions.

Prop setup: N/A.

Action/s: Ensure there is at least one magazine loaded with 1+ dummy rounds to keep yourself from beating the magazine up. (NEVER use live ammunition) Begin by aiming in on the starting target (designated below), and reload while swinging the gun to the next target. You will NOT go through the three normal sets in this drill (TTS, MTTS and "Catch the Timer") just perform one set of 10 MTTS repetitions with each version listed below. On the start signal of the timer, practice reloading while swinging the gun from/to the following positions:

- ➢ 12 to 3 o'clock target and fire one shot. (10 repetitions)
- ➢ 12 to 9 o'clock target and fire one shot. (10 repetitions)
- ➢ 3 to 9 o'clock target and fire one shot. (10 repetitions)
- ➢ 9 to 3 o'clock target and fire one shot. (10 repetitions)

If possible, you can also set up two more targets between the 1-2 and 10-11 o'clock positions and reload while swinging to those targets.

Critical Points: You will have to use a step to get your body into the right position, practice reloading stepping forward and backward. Do not leave the gun fully extended when reloading the gun; bring it back about half the distance of full extension.

Visual Cues: Visual shift should go from the front sight, to the magazine well, back to the target center, and finally back to the front sight again during the reload.

Mental Cues: Actively visualize the entire drill.

By: Mike Seeklander

Table Reload

Type: Reloading	Total Repetitions: 30 +

Purpose: To build the manipulation skill of reloading the gun from a table.

Start position: Gun set up with a magazine inserted (empty or partially full of dummy rounds), hammer/striker cocked, aimed in at the target with the finger in the prepped position.

Target type and setup: One small IPSC set at room distance, one directly in front of the shooter.

Prop setup: Table with flat surface waist high or slightly above.

Action/s: Ensure there is at least on magazine loaded with 1+ dummy rounds to keep yourself from beating the magazine up on the table. (NEVER use live ammunition) Begin by aiming in on the target directly to your front (12 o'clock). On the start signal of the timer, practice reloading from the table and fire one shot.

Critical Points: Make sure to properly index the magazine from the table. Bend your knees to lower your body to the magazine rather than bending over if necessary.

Visual Cues: Visual shift to the magazine on the table is critical to get a good reload, as well as the shift back to the magazine well, and finally back to the target and front sight.

Mental Cues: Actively visualize the entire drill.

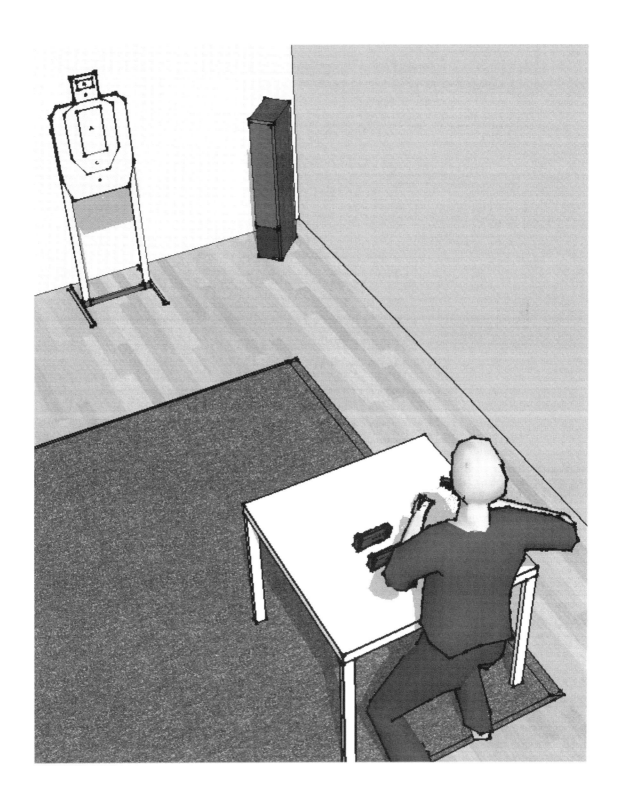

By: Mike Seeklander

Reload and Transfer

Type: Specialty	Total Repetitions: 30 +

Purpose: To build the manipulation skill of reloading the gun and then transferring it the support hand (weak hand).

Start position: Gun set up with an empty magazine, hammer/striker cocked, aimed at the target with the finger in the prepped position.

Target type and setup: One small IPSC set at room distance, one directly in front of the shooter.

Prop setup: N/A.

Action/s: Ensure there is at least one magazine loaded with 1+ dummy rounds to keep yourself from beating the magazine in your magazine pouch. (NEVER use live ammunition) Begin by aiming in on the target directly to your front (12 o'clock). On the start signal of the timer, practice reloading the gun and then transferring to the support hand and firing one shot.

Critical Points: Reload and then transfer, don't try to do both at the same time. Pay particular attention to where the trigger finger is during this reload.

Visual Cues: Visual shift back to the gun when reloading, and transferring. Shift your vision back to the target and then front sight only when the reload/transfer is done.

Mental Cues: Actively visualize the entire drill.

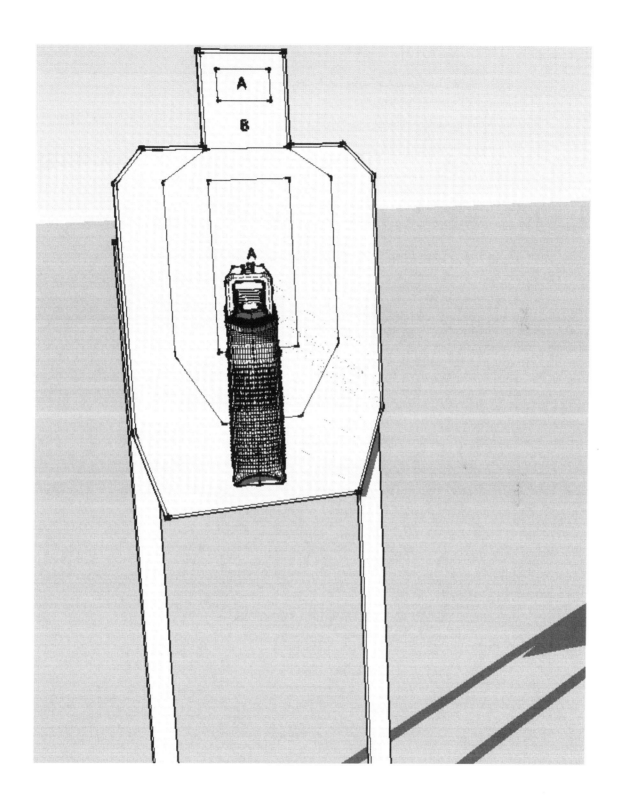

By: Mike Seeklander

IDPA Reloads

Type: Reloading	Total Repetitions: 30 +

Purpose: To build the manipulation skill of reloading the gun with IDPA approved reloads.

Start position:

(Emergency reload) Gun set up with an empty magazine, slide locked to the rear, aimed at the target with the finger in the prepped position. *Or*

(Tactical or retention reload) With a magazine with one or more rounds in the magazine in the gun, aimed in at the target with the finger in the prepped position.

Target type and setup: One small IDPA set at room distance, directly in front of the shooter and barricade.

Prop setup: A simulated or real barricade (I use a IDPA target on a portable stand) set up in a position where you can use it as cover.

Action/s: On the start signal of the timer, practice reloading the gun performing either a slide lock reload or a retention reload of your choice.

Critical Points: Move from one side to the other of the barricade when doing the retention reloads. Make sure to use proper cover (IDPA rules). Find the right area to stow the magazine when doing retention reload (some use a pocket, some stuff it in their pants). Use the same spot consistently.

Visual Cues: Visual shift back to the gun when reloading.

Mental Cues: Actively visualize the entire drill.

By: Mike Seeklander

Target Acquisitions

Type: Specialty	Total Repetitions: 30 +

Purpose: To build the skill of acquiring targets with the gun.

Start position: Gun with hammer back or striker cocked, aimed at the left target in the array, with the finger in the prepped position.

Target type and setup: Two small IPSC set at room distance, far enough apart so you can get a 45-degree swing between the targets if possible.

Prop setup: N/A.

Action/s: On the start signal of the timer, drive the gun hard to the next target, prep and fire one shot. Make sure you are prepping the trigger as you drive the gun into the target area. Now start on that target and practice driving the gun in the other direction (you will have to work the slide to reset the trigger/striker). Your par times should be the same between targets.

Critical Points: Getting off the trigger and re-prepping it as you enter the next target. The trigger should be prepped before you get the gun stopped. Use your legs and core to drive the gun fast to the next target. See visual cues.

Visual Cues: It is important to shift your eyes to the next target and drive the gun behind your eyes. Drive your vision to a specific spot on the target, and that is where the gun will stop. Don't forget to do a visual shift back to the front sight for verification.

Mental Cues: Actively visualize the entire drill.

Copyright 2010 Shooting-Performance   By: Mike Seeklander

Summary: Ok, lets summarize the dry fire program. You will:

☐ Dry fire five days per week, going through
  o Session A on Monday and Thursday
  o Session B on Tuesday and Friday
  o Session C on Wednesday and Saturday (Saturday optional if no match)
☐ Use a PACT or other type timer with the PAR function for two sets:
  o The first set will be at your TTS (Technical Training Speed), which is a speed slower than your maximum, and a pace that you can perform all repetitions perfectly.
  o The second set will be at your MTTS (Maximum Technical Training Speed), which is 100% of you available maximum (as fast as you can perform the drill and still be doing all repetitions correctly)
  o During the third set, once you have done 10 at your MTTS, you will begin to drop the PAR time by either .05 or .10 increments, and attempt to "catch" that time. Catching the time is defined as doing the repetition correctly under the selected PAR time.
  o Once you have caught the time and have done a minimum of 5 repetitions at that new time, try dropping it again. Keep doing this until you fail to catch the time.
  o Record your new MTTS. This is where you will begin the next dry fire session, after you complete your TTS set.
☐ On the movement drills, you might find that you can make the time on certain movements (in the clock drill for example), but not on others. Keep working at it until you can meet the time for every number on the clock.

CHAPTER FOUR
Live Fire
Training Module

"Correct Design and Perfect Execution will be the key to your success"

By: Mike Seeklander

The things I will cover in this chapter:

1. *Skills trained in the live fire program*
2. *Execution of live fire training sessions (pre, during and post session)*
3. *Live fire training drills types*
4. *Live fire training schedule*
5. *Live fire training phases (I, II, and III)*
6. *Breakdown of the three live fire training sessions (A, B, and C)*
7. *Scoring procedures for the drills*

Skills Trained (firing cycle and marksmanship) - The live fire training module will improve your ability to shoot better. The firing cycle is the trigger, sight, and grip management that you must master in order to shoot fast and hit your target. You will have primarily developed your manipulation skills in dry fire, so the focus will be on improving elements of the firing cycle during your live fire sessions. Your live fire training time is better spent if you are focusing on the concepts of improving your ability to hit the target faster and more accurately. Remember, you will work on your manipulation skills primarily in dry fire sessions.

Execution (performing live fire training) - Your live fire training sessions will be a big key in this training program. I want you to follow these guidelines as closely as possible. There are three separate timeframes in each live fire training session: *pre-session*, *during-session*, and *post-session*. Because you will be tying everything together (mental and physical) it is important for you to understand what should be done in each area. Here are the timeframes, as well as your actions in each of them:

> ➢ *Pre-session*
>> ▪ *Mental toughness routine-* To get ready for your training session you will start with a short piece of mental work that will increase your mental connection to the drills. This short exercise will help

build your self-image and mental toughness, and since you will do it for each session, you will consistently build your mental strengths *while* you are building your technical skills. This routine is a combination of exercises[4] that I have found to be simple yet effective, and will be a big key to your success, so don't skip it. The details of your mental toughness routine are in the "Mental Toughness Training" section.

- *Review and prepare-* This is the review of your notes, and preparation of your gear. I usually read over my notes from my last training session while I am prepping my magazines and putting on my gear. DO NOT skip this step. Your notes to yourself from your last session are critical and will greatly increase the effectiveness of the current session. Look for things you had problems with, as well as the times and hits that you scored on the last drills. You should always be trying to beat your last session, so it is a good idea to carry over those key times to the current log page (maybe in the notes section). Also, go ahead and fill out the general details on your log sheet for the current session. This includes things such as the weather, gear, etc.

- *Target and prop setup-* After review and preparation, you should be ready to look over the current session plan and set up for your first drill. The drills in the training sessions in this program are in an order that will increase your learning experience as well as be easier and faster to set up and perform if you follow the order I have them assigned. If for some reason you have to skip a drill,

---

[4] Jason Selk, <u>10-Minute Toughness</u> (New York: McGraw-Hill, 2004).

85

note why and move on. If you have to modify a drill because of a range or prop restriction, go ahead and change it, but be sure you note how you changed it so you can set it up the same way next time. This will keep your tracking metrics the same so you can validate your progress. If you need help modifying a drill and are unsure of the effect of changing them, don't hesitate to get in touch with me.

- ➢ *During session*
  - ▪ *Visualization-* I will cover this in more detail in the next section, but as a reminder, - you will actively visualize the drill before you do it each time. When shooting matches, we use active visualization to create a successful pathway in our memory allowing us to perform our plan, so it only makes sense that you "practice" active visualization during your training sessions. Doing active visualization will help you improve your ability to see yourself perform well, and then actually perform well.
  - ▪ *Video-* I highly recommend you use video in your documentation, and make sure to set up the video camera in a position where it will capture the key details of the drill you are about to perform. For example, if I am executing a movement drill, I will want to make sure the camera captures my entire body from an angle that shows me throughout the drill. I usually set my camera up far enough away so that I can see my footwork at about the 2-4 o'clock position. Don't shoot the camera.
  - ▪ *Execute and document (written and video)-* So, you have done everything including setting up for the drill. You have hopefully actively visualized the drill by now and have seen yourself do it. It

is now time to do it. Set your logbook in a place where you can quickly write down the times for each repetition. You will count your points on the target after you have done all repetitions. Load your gun and execute the drill. Try to keep your loading process the same process you will use at a match, and begin creating consistent habits now. Make sure to write down times for each repetition and keep notes if something goes right or wrong. I log all repetitions that I am doing if they are part of a drill. If you are group shooting or testing some ammunition or whatever, don't worry about logging that unless there is something you want to remember. Pay attention to this critical point: Each repetition of the drill must be performed as perfect as you can. You will write your subconscious programs here, and if written wrong you will get wrong when you try to apply those skills under pressure. When I am going through my training repetitions, I shoot the drill as fast as I can while still in control. Then I begin pushing the pace and trying to go faster, while maintaining control. This is what you should be doing, always trying to expand your "control zone" by trying to go faster and faster while maintaining correctness. Once you begin to make mistakes, or the hits begin to get bad, back off and regain your control. Then begin to push again. Another key is to stop and correct mistakes mentally before you push on. What this means is that during my training repetitions, if I make a mistake, I will stop and analyze the mistake, and then correct it in my mind (by running a correct visualization) before I begin again. Sometimes you will have to stop and focus on one area in a drill, to correct something small that you are doing wrong. The point is

87

that you must stop, mentally correct it, and then begin your training repetitions again and physically make yourself do the technique right.

- *Scoring*- Once you are done with all repetitions for the specific drill, unload and make a safe weapon and go check your hits. Count total hits on the target to ensure you have not missed, and then count total points (scoring will mimic the divisions you shoot). Log your total points on your log sheet.

> *Post session*

- *Document and review*- Now it is time to capture the rest of what occurred in your training session, such as what you did well and what you need to work on in future sessions. If you use the log sheets in *Your Performance Logbook*, they will force you to write down all details you will need to capture. (Why not use the logbook I use? For more information on "Your Performance Logbook", see my website) Once you have finished logging all data, take the time and figure out any scoring metrics (such as hit factor) and write them down.

Live Fire Training Schedule - You will be doing three different live fire sessions on the range. With this program, I want you to perform each of the three sessions once per week, but for those of you who are more or less aggressive in your program I have a simple solution for you to train less or more. The minimum I recommend is three times per week if you want to see some big improvement, but it is ok to do less if you have too. Another important thing to remember: if you miss a training session pick it up the next time you train, don't skip over it.

Here are your scheduling options:

Standard Option (this is what I recommend for most people): You will go through each of the sessions once per week. The actual days you do these sessions could vary, but this is a great split that allows you to train every other day, and hit a match on Saturday.

Sun	Mon	Tue	Wed	Thu	Fri	Sat
Off	Session A	Off	Session B	Off	Session C	Match

Intensive Option (this is for those who want to reach the top faster and have the time to do so): You will go through each session once, and then repeat the core sessions A and B again during a week. If you actually had the time and resources, you could train twice a day a couple days per week too, and once on a single day. Be careful though, training more than once per day may lead to mental burnout and physical overtraining (shooting can take a toll on tendons and ligaments in the hands and arms).

Sun	Mon	Tue	Wed	Thu	Fri	Sat
Off	Session A	Session B	Session C	Session A	Session B	Match

Alternate Option: This is designed for someone who can only train (live fire) twice a week, which is the absolute minimum I recommend. You are going to rotate through the sessions: Rotate A, B, C, A, B, C, etc.

Sun	Mon	Tue	Wed	Thu	Fri	Sat
Off	Session A	Off	Off	Session B	Off	Match
Off	Session C	Off	Off	Session A	Off	OFF

By: Mike Seeklander

3 Separate Training Phases - The training drills will all be done following three separate phases each differing in length (because each have different timeframes required to learn the skills). They will vary from four to six weeks in length (4, 6, and 6 respectively). To go through the entire skills training program once will take eighteen weeks (sixteen weeks with two off weeks), and after that you will have the option to use the drills that you need the most based on your observations and modification of your program. As stated before, you will want to start the skills training program on a date that will allow you to finish it at least a month before your big event. All three phases may incorporate similar drills, however Phases II and III will have increased distance and skill requirements. After each phase you will take one full week off (from dry fire and live fire) to regroup, reassess, and refocus.

This chart gives you an overview of the Training Phases concept.

Live Fire Training Phases

Phase One-	Phase Two-	Phase Three-
This phase will be spent developing fundamentals.	This phase will be spent on putting the fundamentals together.	This phase will be the hardest and longest and will primarily be made up of harder, Macro drills.
Easy Distance/skills	Medium Distance/skills	Hard Distance/skills

During each Phase, you will be following one of three different daily training plans each time you train. They are as follows:

*A – **Fundamental Skills**- This session is designed to work your fundamental firing cycle skills.*

*B – **Movement Skills**- This session focuses elements of the firing cycle, while moving. This session teaches you how to patiently wait for the sights to settle before firing the gun.*

*C – **Specialty Skills**- This session focuses on the specialty skills we use in USPSA/IDPA.*

*An overview of the drills contained in each session during **PHASE ONE:***

Session	Session A (Fundamentals)	RDS	Session B (Movement)	RDS	Session C (Specialty)	RDS
Drill's	**ALL SESSIONS WILL BEGIN WITH THE FIVE ROUND WARM UP DRILL**					
	Extending (toward) Prep and Press	40	Pivoting Draw Drill/Varied Target Area (clock drill)	48	Strong and Support Hand Transfer	60
	Horizontal (L-R) Prep and Press	45	Moving Draw/Varied Target Area (clock drill)	48	Draw, Reload and Transfer	60
	Static Draw/ Varied Target Area	40	Shooting and Moving, Forward and Backward	120	Multi-Port Drill	80
	Static Reload/Varied Target Area	48				
	Long Range Challenge	60				
Total Rounds	**233**		**216**		**200**	

91

By: Mike Seeklander

*An overview of the drills contained in each session during **PHASE TWO:***

Session	Session A (fundamentals)	RDS	Session B (Movement)	RDS	Session C (Specialty)	RDS
Drill's	ALL SESSIONS WILL BEGIN WITH THE FIVE ROUND WARM UP DRILL					
	1 shot X-Drill	48	Short Movement into Position	50	Multi-Position Drill	40
	2 shot X-Drill	80	Long Movement into Position	60	Strong and Weak Hand X-Drill	80
	Acceleration/Dec-eleration	50	Shooting and Moving Multidirectional	90	Long Range Challenge II	60
	Multi-Hardcover Drill	40			Off Balance Shooting	40
Total Rounds	218		200		220	

*An overview of the drills contained in each session during **PHASE THREE:***

Session	Session A (fundamentals)	RDS	Session B (Movement)	RDS	Session C (Specialty)	RDS
Drill's	ALL SESSIONS WILL BEGIN WITH THE FIVE ROUND WARM UP DRILL					
	1 shot X-Drill (phase 3)	48	Shooting and Moving, Aggressive Entry	60	Strong and Weak Hand X-Drill (phase 3)	40
	2 shot X-Drill (phase 3)	80	Shooting and Moving Multidirectional	90	Multi-Port Drill	40
	Barricade X-Drill	80	Moving Reload	60	Long Range Challenge III	60
	Multiple Distance with Reload	60			Target Acquisition	50
Total Rounds	268		210		190	

<u>Live Fire Training Drills</u> - You will be utilizing two primary drill types, Micro and Macro during your training sessions. Micro drills are exactly what the word implies, small drills with a focus on a small area of skill. Macro drills are larger drills with more complex skills trained, usually a combination of skills that are tied together. I use Micro drills to work on small components of skill and Macro drills to train the concept of tying multiple individual skills together, as well as integrating the mental side of the game through visualization. The concept of "flowing" seamlessly from one technique to the next can be trained by the use of Macro drills. When you reflect upon your notes from training or game day, the mistakes you find will usually be small things that you must focus all of your mental attention on when correcting. For this purpose, you will use Micro drills since they allow you to really focus on a single component of a technique. In order to refine technique to the mastery level, you will have to look at every detail of every skill and constantly train those areas moving toward perfection of your technique. One last thing, each training session will begin with the 5 shot warm up drill, to ensure that your gun is zeroed and ammunition that you are shooting is performing like you expect. Shooting these groups tests both your fundamentals, as well as takes any excuses away for shooting errors during the drill.

Note: *The next section lists the Shooting-Performance Competitive Training Drill Sheets, as well as general instructions that will help you use them properly. Remember, these drills are all designed to work certain key skills and they have a specific design so follow them exactly as they are written. If you start to modify the drills, then the next time you train you will have NOTHING to compare because the drill was done differently each time you trained.*

93

Drill types. The training drills are broken down into Micro and Macro drills. Each drill is designed to work a specific area of skill. Micro drills focus on one or two small portions of a technique. Macro drills are larger drills where the skills are mixed together to work on flowing from one technique to the next while performing all techniques correctly.

Required Equipment. The training drills are designed to be very simple in nature, and require very little to actually do them. I designed them so the average shooter, with little range gear could use them without having to buy expensive steel targets, or specialized stuff. You will need, at a minimum, the following:

  ➢ Targets (IPSC or IDPA), standard are preferred (not classic turtle targets)
  ➢ Pasters (brown and black)
  ➢ Paint (white)
  ➢ One 8 or 10 inch steel plate (free standing) or a small pepper popper (resetting is preferred)
  ➢ (5) Target stands (I have used the folding ones made by GT and they work fine, but any design will work)
  ➢ Target sticks (lathe) to staple targets to
  ➢ Stapler and staples
  ➢ (13) Small orange cones or small marking disks (the small disks that you can press into the ground are great)
  ➢ (2) Barrels (the large plastic ones are preferred), these can be substituted with 5-10 gallon buckets or anything similar, or even orange traffic cones.

Starting Distance. Each drill has a starting distance in the main body. This distance is for shooters that are beginners or classified in the lower classes of IDPA or USPSA/IPSC (D-C classes or Novice-Marksman). Those who begin the program at a more advanced level will use the alternate "advanced distances" that are in the bottom section of the drill. IF YOU VARY THE DISTANCE, MAKE SURE YOU DOCUMENT IT IN YOUR TRAINING LOG.

Alternating Target Area. Several of the drills require the shooter to alternate between target areas (head and body A or 0 zones). This is to work the skill at two different paces. Those who are training with the Classic (turtle) targets will just use the center A zone since there is no head on these targets. When doing the drills, shooters MUST accept that there will be a significant difference in the pace they can hit the upper A zone (or head for IDPA) and the body A zone (or 0 for IDPA).

By: Mike Seeklander

Sections. Each drill is broken down into different sections. These sections will give you all of the information you will need to successfully execute the drills.

Targets. Unless otherwise noted, all targets for drills are 5' high at the shoulder or top of turtle target. (Use standard IPSC as primary training target, which may be substituted with an IDPA target if desired).

Shooting Sport. Some of you will be using this program for USPSA/IPSC and some of you will be training for IDPA. Each drill is designed with an IDPA option (some of them require no modification) that will guide you in changing the drill to make it IDPA friendly.

Equipment. Gun and related gear should be legal within the division you plan to shoot the most. Load to division capacity and do reloads where necessary on the Macro drills unless otherwise noted on the drill. Micro drills as well as most Macro drills will not require a slide lock (emergency) reload unless you are training for IDPA, in which case you should train primarily slide lock reloads.

Consistency. It is incredibly important that you keep things consistent when doing these drills. Failures to do so will result in times and hits that are not trackable or measurable. The goal is to measure the metrics of the drills as you evolve and watch your progress, always driving your skill to the next level.

Scoring/Tracking. Scoring and tracking of drills should be done consistently and will take place by doing the following
  ➢ Document the times for each drill repetition, and anything noteworthy.
  ➢ After the prescribed number of repetitions has taken place, count total hits on the target, and well as hits in each zone.
  ➢ Scoring should be done for whatever sport you are competing in (IDPA or IPSC) as follows:
    o IPSC: Total points (subtract 10 for each miss/penalty) / Total Time (add times together) = Hit factor
    o IDPA: Total time + (Points dropped * .5 seconds) = Total time (or score)
  ➢ Paste the target and get set up for the next drill.
  ➢ Note: Sometimes I just paste non-A or 0 hits, and leave the holes in the center of the target, to save time. You can do this if you like, and are at the level where you KNOW if you are missing the target. A side benefit is that having holes in the target already forces you to call bad shots from the sight picture (sight alignment or dot), versus looking for hits (a bad habit) as you are shooting.

Five Shot Warm Up

Rounds Per Repetition	5	Total Rounds	
			15+
Total Repetitions		**Accuracy and Time Goals**	**Group**
	3+		

Purpose: To verify gun/ammunition combination is shooting point of aim, point of impact, by shooting a group on a specific spot. To verify basic mechanics on the process of sight and trigger management. Once you verify the gun is shooting where we want it to, with the ammunition you are training with, analysis of other training factors is easier (i.e. you don't blame the gun for a bad shot).

Start position: IPSC Ready (where hands meet after draw).

Target type and setup: Standard IPSC @ 10 yards, centered on the shooter, with a 2x2 piece of black tape or a black paster.

Prop setup: N/A

Action/s: With no time limitations, shoot 3 groups, using the following guidelines:

> First group of five shots, fire as slowly and accurately as possible. Assess group for size, and position. Repeat if necessary. Fliers should be noted and called when shot.

> Second group of five shots, fire at controlled competition speed (as fast as you can hit the tape/paster. Look for a group shift from the slow fire group.

> Third group of five shots, fire each shot after extending the gun from the IPSC ready. Assess group for shift from the slow fire group.

Critical Points: Touch trigger program, building a proper grip, follow through and reset.

Visual Cues: Focal shift from front target center, to front sight.

Mental Cues: Actively visualize the entire drill.

Advanced Distance: Increase distance to 15 yards

Phase 3: N/A

IDPA Option: N/A

By: Mike Seeklander

Extending (toward) Prep and Press

Rounds Per Repetition	2	Total Rounds	
			40
Total Repetitions		**Accuracy and Time Goals**	**90%** A's, no D's
	20		

Purpose: To work on the touch trigger mental program (touch trigger/shift visual focus from the target to sights) and elements of the firing cycle using an ACP (accelerated competition pull) and CCP (controlled competition pull) trigger management, as well as the development of a strong, neutral grip.

Start position: IPSC Ready [IR] (where hands meet after draw).

Target type and setup: Standard IPSC @ 10 yards, centered on the shooter.

Prop setup: N/A

Action/s: From IR on the sound of the timer, extend the gun while prepping the trigger and running the touch trigger program (visual shift and verification), fire two shots. Repeat the same drill during the next repetition, alternating and using the upper A/B/0 target zone. You will go through the firing cycle for each shot.

Critical Points: Touch trigger program, building a proper grip, follow through and reset.

Visual Cues: Start focused on the center of the A zone. Focal shift from front target center, to front sight.

Mental Cues: Actively visualize the entire drill.

Advanced Distance: Increase distance to 15 yards

Phase 3: N/A

IDPA Option: N/A

10 Yds

By: Mike Seeklander

Horizontal (L-R) Prep and Press

Rounds Per Repetition	3	Total Rounds	
			45
Total Repetitions		Accuracy and Time Goals	90% A's, no D's
	15		

Purpose: To work on the touch trigger mental program (touch trigger/shift visual focus from the target to sights) and elements of the firing cycle using an ACP (accelerated competition pull) and CCP (controlled competition pull) trigger management while driving the gun horizontally.

Start position: IPSC Ready [IR] (where hands meet after draw).

Target type and setup: Two (2) Standard IPSC 10 yards away 5 yards apart.

Prop setup: N/A

Action/s: Center yourself between the targets. From IR on the sound of the timer, extend the gun toward the left target, prepping the trigger while running the touch trigger program (visual shift and verification), fire the shot and reset and prep while driving the gun to the right target body A/O zone, fire one shot, and then drive the gun back to the left target and fire one shot on the upper (head) A/B/0 zone. Return to IPSC Ready and repeat for the remaining repetitions.

Critical Points: Touch trigger program, building a proper grip, follow through (call the shot before driving to the next target) and reset. MAKE UP SHOTS!

Visual Cues: Focal shift from front target center, to front sight.

Mental Cues: Actively visualize the entire drill.

Advanced Distance: Increase distance to 15 yards.

Phase 3: N/A.

IDPA Option: N/A

5 Yds

10 Yds

101

By: Mike Seeklander

Static Draw / Varied Target Area

Rounds Per Repetition	2	Total Rounds	
			40
Total Repetitions		**Accuracy and Time Goals**	**90%** A's, no D's
	20		

Purpose: To work on the static draw and firing cycle components to varied target areas.

Start position: Holstered, hands relaxed at sides

Target type and setup: One (1) standard IPSC target at 7 yards

Prop setup: N/A

Action/s: On the timer, draw and fire two shots to the body A zone, re-holster. On the next timer beep, draw and fire two shots to the upper A zone (or head for IDPA).

Critical Points: Index points while gripping the gun, and forming the grip.

Visual Cues: Focal point should be exactly where you want to hit, and the focus should shift from that point to the front sight as the front sight comes into view during extension.

Mental Cues: React quickly to the timer beep.

Advanced Distance: Increase distance to 10 yards

Phase 3: N/A

IDPA Option: Utilize cover garment.

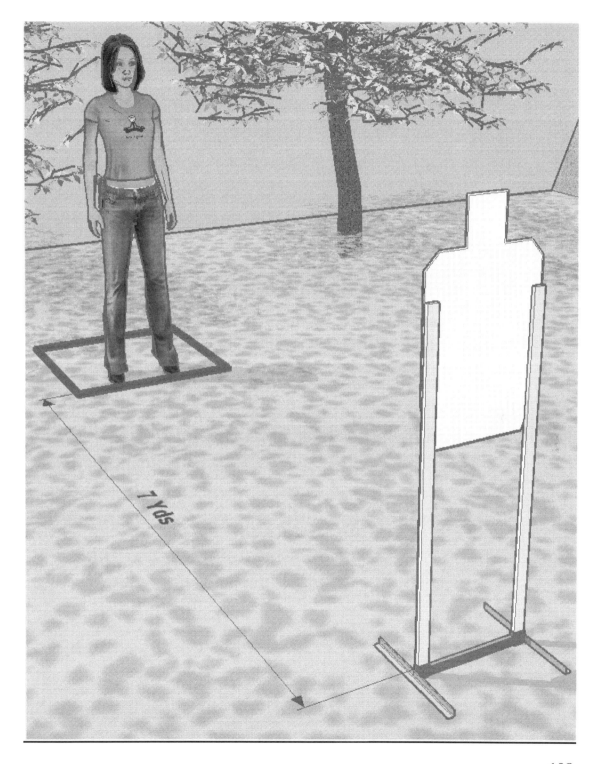

7 Yds

By: Mike Seeklander

Pivoting Draw Drill/ Varied Target Area

Rounds Per Repetition	2	Total Rounds	
			48
Total Repetitions	24	Accuracy and Time Goals	90% A's, no D's

Purpose: To work on the pivoting draw and firing cycle components to varied target areas.

Start position: Holstered, hands relaxed at sides

Target type and setup: One (1) standard IPSC target at 7 yards

Prop setup: N/A

Action/s: Start by facing an imaginary 1'oclock if you were standing in the middle of the clock (your head and eyes should face whatever clock position each time). On the timer, pivot, draw and fire two shots to the body A zone, re-holster. Now face 2 o'clock and on the next timer beep, pivot, draw and fire two shots to the upper A zone (or head for IDPA). Continue to work your way around the clock, and continue alternating target areas. Work around the clock twice (obviously do not start at 12 o'clock since there would be no pivot), using the pivoting pivot and the stepping pivot. When you are at the 6 o'clock position, practice one turn left and one turn right (to practice both even though pivoting on our gun side is preferred). Total repetitions around the clock will be 12 due to the two directions at 6 o'clock.

Critical Points: Head and eye movement to the target when the timer goes off (the body will follow).

Visual Cues: Focal point should be exactly where you want to hit, and the focus should shift from that point to the front sight as the front sight comes into view during extension.

Mental Cues: React quickly to the timer beep.

Advanced Distance: Increase distance to 10 yards

Phase 3: N/A

IDPA Option: N/A

Credit Goes To: N/A

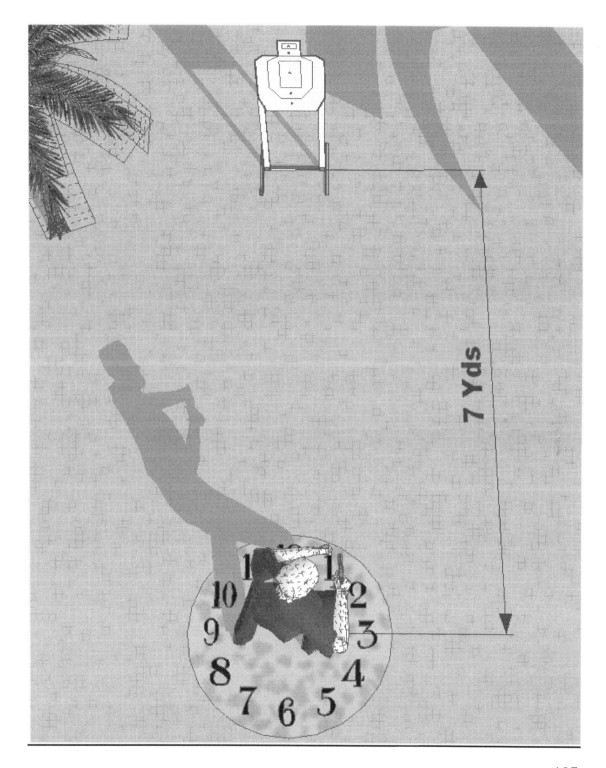

7 Yds

By: Mike Seeklander

Moving Draw/Varied Target Area (Clock Drill)

Rounds Per Repetition	2	Total Rounds	48
Total Repetitions	24	Accuracy and Time Goals	**90%** A's, no D's

Purpose: To work on applying proper firing cycle components while stepping into positions. To improve footwork.

Start position: Holstered, hands relaxed at sides

Target type and setup: One (1) standard IPSC target at 7 yards

Prop setup: Markers or cones set at each number on a clock and one marker on the center position of the clock. Each number marker should be 2 yards (2 paces) away from the center position.

Action/s: First designate a stepping foot (you will go around the entire clock stepping toward each number with both feet). Start in the center of the clock and on the timer beep, draw and step with the appropriate foot toward the positions on the clock starting with 12 o'clock, and fire two shots. Lead foot will step toward clock position, and the rear will follow. You will be cross stepping when stepping opposite of the stepping foot you are using (for example stepping to the left side of the clock with the right foot). Alternate target areas each repetition from the body A zone to the upper A zone. International shooters using the turtle (diamond) target should just use the body A zone.   Each step should be treated as one repetition of the exercise. Work around the clock twice, one time with each foot designated as the stepping foot.

Critical Points: Gun stabilization, *while* stepping in. Enter low and stay low, don't stand up while shooting. Work on shooting earlier, allowing the sights to settle. The foot that hits the ground first will have most of the weight on it during the movement, and the other foot should settle softly so that it does not disturb the sights.

Visual Cues: Patiently wait for the sights to settle.

Mental Cues: Actively visualize the entire drill.

Advanced Distance: Increase distance to 10 yards.

Phase 3: N/A

IDPA Option: Utilize a cover garment.

By: Mike Seeklander

Static Reload / Varied Target Area

Rounds Per Repetition	4	Total Rounds	
			48
Total Repetitions		**Accuracy and Time Goals**	**90%** A's, no D's
	12		

Purpose: To work on the static reload. To work on applying proper firing cycle components before and after the reload.

Start position: Holstered, hands relaxed at sides

Target type and setup: One (1) standard IPSC target at 7 yards

Prop setup: N/A

Action/s: On the timer beep, draw and fire two shots to the body A zone, perform a reload, and fire two more shots to the upper A zone. On the next repetition, start on the upper A zone, reload, and fire two shots to the body A zone. Continue to alternate target areas. If training for IDPA, set the gun up for and perform a slide lock reload.

Critical Points: Make sure to shoot the head shots with a pace that will guarantee hits. Misses are unacceptable. Reload position, fast/slow/fast concept, looking at the proper index point (the magazine well).

Visual Cues: Eye shift from the target, to the magazine well, back to the target (after the magazine begins its insertion into the magazine well).

Mental Cues: Actively visualize the entire drill.

Advanced Distance: Increase distance to 10 yards

Phase 3: N/A

IDPA Option: Utilize cover garment.

7 Yds

109

By: Mike Seeklander

Moving Reload

Rounds Per Repetition	4	Total Rounds	
			60
Total Repetitions		Accuracy and Time Goals	90% A's, no D's
	15		

Purpose: To work on reloading while stepping into positions.

Start position: Holstered, hands relaxed at sides

Target type and setup: One (1) standard IPSC target at 7 yards.

Prop setup: Markers or cones set at each number on a clock and one marker on the center position of the clock. Each number marker should be 2 yards (2 paces) away from the center position.

Action/s: Standing in the absolute center (near your center mark), when the timer goes off draw and fire two shots to the body A zone, reload while stepping to the 12-oclock position and fire two more shots to the upper A zone. Continue to alternate target areas on each repetition. Begin in the center each time and move toward the next position on the clock when reloading. Work your way around the clock. You can use either a single or cross-step while moving as this drill will teach you how to reload while moving out of a position. Each step should be treated as one repetition of the exercise.

Critical Points: The reload should be done as you settle the second foot down (within two steps) Verify proper index of the magazine, as well as the gun to magazine well relationship. Practice the concept of fast/slow/fast when doing the reload. Rebuild the proper grip on the handgun.

Visual Cues: Visual shift from target to magazine well to target.

Mental Cues: Actively visualize the entire drill.

Advanced Distance: Increase distance to 10 yards

Phase 3: N/A

IDPA Option: Utilize a cover garment. Perform IDPA reloads.

7 Yds

111

By: Mike Seeklander

Strong and Support Hand Transfer

Rounds Per Repetition	4	Total Rounds	
			60
Total Repetitions	15	Accuracy and Time Goals	90% A's, no D's

Purpose: To work on building the grip and applying proper firing cycle components with the strong and support hand after the transfer.

Start position: Holstered, hands relaxed at sides.

Target type and setup: One (1) standard IPSC target at 7 yards.

Prop setup: N/A.

Action/s: On the timer, draw, transfer to the support hand and fire two shots to the body A zone, then transfer to the strong hand and fire two shots to the same area.

Critical Points: Proper gun transfer. Gun extension, and stabilization by locking the wrist tendon and grip. Make sure to get the arm behind the gun, and the weight behind the arm. Pay particular attention to prepping the trigger and waiting until the gun movement stabilizes enough to get the hit.

Visual Cues: Visual shift to the gun grip when transferring it (if you look at it when transferring) Patiently wait for the sights to settle.

Mental Cues: Actively visualize the entire drill.

Advanced Distance: Increase distance to 10 yards

Phase 3: Alternate between target areas, for example: draw and fire two to the upper A zone, transfer, and fire two to the body A zone. Then start on the opposite target area on the next repetition.

IDPA Option: Utilize a cover garment.

7 Yds

　　　　　　　　By: Mike Seeklander

Draw, Reload and Transfer

Rounds Per Repetition	4	Total Rounds	
			60
Total Repetitions		**Accuracy and Time Goals**	**90%** A's, no D's
	15		

Purpose: To work on building the grip and applying proper firing cycle components with the strong and support hand after the reload and transfer.

Start position: Holstered, hands relaxed at sides.

Target type and setup: One (1) standard IPSC target at 7 yards.

Prop setup: N/A.

Action/s: On the timer, draw and fire two shots on the target freestyle, reload and transfer to the support hand and fire two more shots.   All shots will be to the body A zone.

Critical Points: Gun extension, and stabilization by locking the wrist tendon and grip!!

Visual Cues: Visual shift to the grip while transferring. Visual shift to the magazine well when reloading. Patiently wait for the sights to settle.

Mental Cues: Actively visualize the entire drill.

Advanced Distance: Increase distance to 10 yards

Phase 3: Alternate between target areas, for example: draw and fire two to the upper A zone, transfer, and fire two to the body A zone. Then start on the opposite target area on the next repetition.

IDPA Option: Utilize cover garment.

7 yds

By: Mike Seeklander

Off Balance Shooting

Rounds Per Repetition	2	Total Rounds	
			40
Total Repetitions		**Accuracy and Time Goals**	**90%** A's, no D's
	20		

Purpose: To work on applying proper firing cycle components while off balance.

Start position: Holstered, hands relaxed at sides.

Target type and setup: One (1) standard IPSC target at 7 yards.

Prop setup: One stick at least as high as the top of your head (DO NOT USE METAL in case you accidentally shoot the stick!). The stick should be one yard in front of your shooting position (feet).

Action/s: Line up the right foot 4 inches left of the stick. On a timer, draw and extend the gun, while shifting your weight and leaning around the stick and fire two shots. Do not move your feet! Repeat ten times and then switch sides by lining up the opposite foot and leaning the opposite direction. (This drill can be done without a stick, simulating the off balance lean).

Critical Points: Lower the center of gravity! Watch the gun recoil and recover.

Visual Cues: Pay attention to how the gun tracks when tilted. Patiently wait for the sights to settle.

Mental Cues: Actively visualize the entire drill.

Advanced Distance: Increase distance to 10 yards

Phase 3: N/A

IDPA Option: Utilize cover garment.

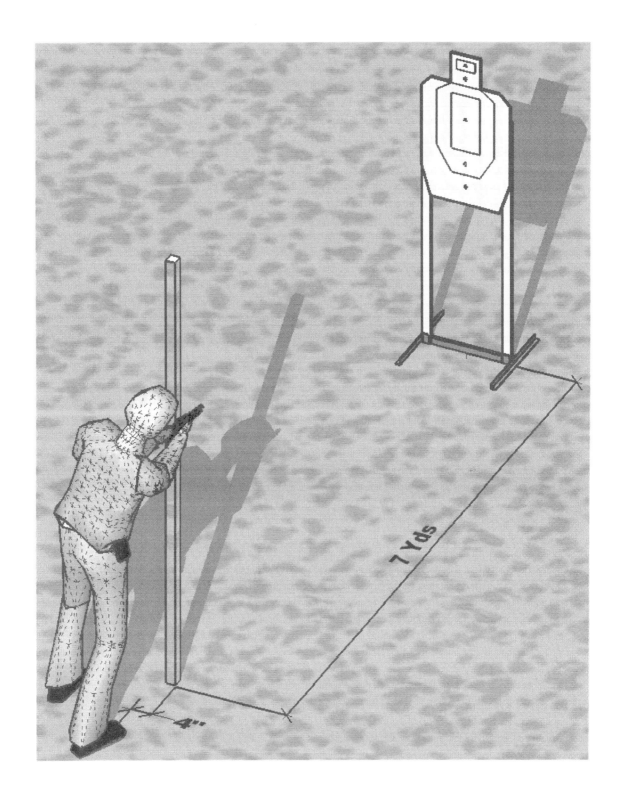

4"

7 Yds

By: Mike Seeklander

Macro Training Drills

Multiple Distance with Reload

Rounds Per Repetition	12	Total Rounds	
			60
Total Repetitions	**5**	**Accuracy and Time Goals**	**90%** A's, no D's

Purpose: To work on the important points of the firing cycle and all fundamental aspects of marksmanship.

Start position: Holstered, hands relaxed at sides.

Target type and setup: 3 IPSC, set at 11, 3, and 18 (left to right) yards directly in front of the shooter with three yards between targets (measured as if they were on line).

Prop setup: N/A

Action/s: On the sound of the timer, draw and fire 2 rounds on each target in this order: T1, T2, then T3, reload and fire two more rounds on each target. Shoot each target as fast as you can guarantee hits (closest should be most aggressive and farthest least aggressive)

Critical Points: Accelerate when you can, and decelerate when you have to. Drive the gun hard between targets (move it fast).

Mental Cues: Actively visualize the entire drill.

Visual Cues: Focal points for the close and far shots (hard focus, soft focus).

Advanced Distances: Increase of targets to 15, 3, and 20 (left to right)

Phase 3: Increase distance to 18, 3, and 25

IDPA Option: Utilize cover garment.

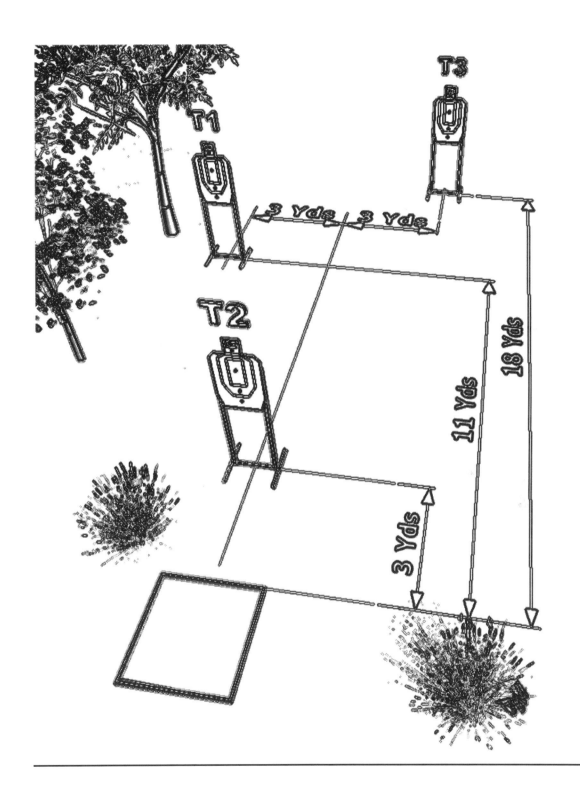

T1

T3

T2

3 Yds 3 Yds

18 Yds

11 Yds

3 Yds

By: Mike Seeklander

Acceleration/Deceleration

Rounds Per Repetition	10	Total Rounds	50
Total Repetitions	5	Accuracy and Time Goals	**90%** A's, no D's

Purpose: To work on applying proper firing cycle components while accelerating, decelerating, and while off balance on a hard target.

Start position: Holstered, hands relaxed or in surrender position

Target type and setup: 3 standard IPSC targets, and an 8-10 inch steel plate. Set two targets and the plate at 20 yards from the start position with the plate in the center (5' high at the shoulders and 3 yards between targets). Set the other target directly in front of the starting position 3 yards away. Ensure you cannot see the plate when in the start position (you will have to step or lean to hit it) and that you don't have any shoot through's on the close target to the far targets.

Prop setup: N/A

Action/s: Draw and fire two on the close target, lean out to the left and fire two shots on the far left target and one on the plate (confirm hit), transition back to the close target and fire two more, and then lean out to the right and fire two shots on the right target and one on the plate (confirm hit). Production guns should start with 11 in the gun to ensure the focus is on getting the hits without having to do an extra load. Make up misses on the steel.

Critical Points: A definitive acceleration/deceleration on the close and far targets. Failure to accelerate on the close target will cost time. Failure to decelerate on the far target will compromise hits. One shot, one hit on the steel is the key, and it is critical that you do what is necessary to hit it (on the first shot). Build follow through and call the hit, making up as necessary.

Mental Cues: Actively visualize the entire drill. Mental key is the hit on steel.

Visual Cues: Focal points for the close and far shots (hard focus, soft focus). A visual reference and pause on the steel target.

Advanced Distance: N/A

Phase 3: Add a reload and repeat the same sequence.

IDPA Option: Utilize cover garment.

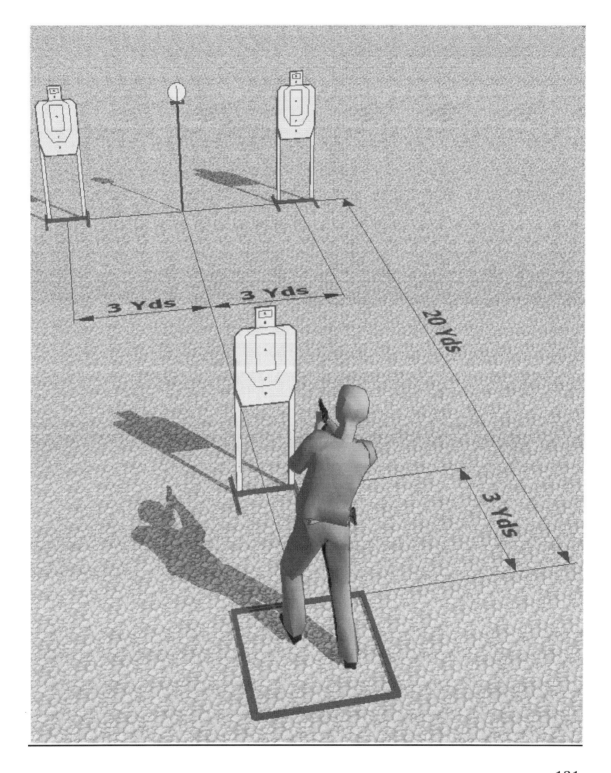

3 Yds   3 Yds   20 Yds   3 Yds

121

Copyright 2010 Shooting-Performance   By: Mike Seeklander

Short Movement Into Position

Rounds Per Repetition	10	Total Rounds	50
Total Repetitions	5	Accuracy and Time Goals	90% A's, no D's

Purpose: To work on short movement into position, and the use of stage markers.

Start position: Standing, aiming at the target, with the finger near or on the trigger (prepped), simulating that you just got done shooting that target.

Target type and setup: 2 IPSC at 10 yards with 2 yards between them.

Prop setup: Two Barricades pushed together (or 3 IPSC targets stapled side by side) 9 yards from the targets. The barricade (or targets) will be a vision barrier. Make or find small marks on the left and right sides of the barrier, that is exactly where the gun would have to be (the same height) when shooting the target on that side (this is called a stage marker and will help you get into position to shoot faster)

Action/s: Start on the left hand side of the vision barrier in view of the left target. On the timer, drive the gun toward the stage marker (see technique section for definition) you have found on the right hand side of the vision barrier, and move into that position. Do not collapse the arms when moving to a position. Fire two shots at the right target when the gun settles, and immediately drive the gun/body to the left position, and fire two shots to the left target. Alternate back and forth until you have fired 10 rounds (you should end on the opposite side you started).

Critical Points: Due to the short movement, both hands stay on the gun, and stay extended. Do not waste time by collapsing the arms. Keep your body weight on the foot that you enter the position with, and lightly settle the trailing foot. Stabilize the gun and press through the trigger when the sights settle (accept some wobble/movement). Keep distance from the barricade (don't get sucked in).

Mental Cues: Actively visualize the entire drill.

Visual Cues: Keep the gun just below vision level until entering the box. Find the stage marker with your vision and drive the gun toward it when moving from one position.

Advanced Distance: N/A

Phase 3: N/A

IDPA Option: Utilize cover garment, and cover per IDPA rules.

Credit Goes To: Phil Strader (www.straightersolutions.com)

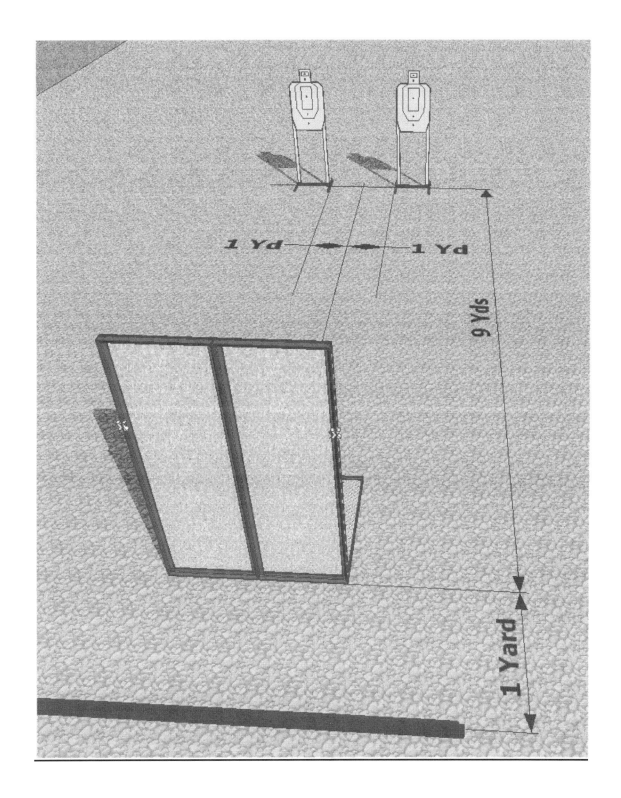

1 Yd ◄ ► 1 Yd

9 Yds

1 Yard

123

By: Mike Seeklander

Long Movement Into Position

Rounds Per Repetition	12	Total Rounds	60
Total Repetitions	5	Accuracy and Time Goals	**90%** A's, no D's

Purpose: To work on the important points of entering and exiting positions, as well as proper body movement in positions and the use of stop markers.

Start position: Holstered, hands relaxed at sides.

Target type and setup: 4 IPSC, 2 sets of 2 at 10 yards with one set directly in front of each shooting box. There should be two feet between the targets, and 5 yards between sets.

Prop setup: Three shooting boxes, two centered on the target arrays, 10 yards from the targets. The third will be centered on the left array, at 15 yards.

Action/s: Starting in the 15 yard left box, draw (on the buzz of a timer) and explode to the first box in front of you. Since there is 5 yards between the boxes, you will dismount and then remount the gun 1-2 steps before you enter. Enter the box with the gun high, and shoot both targets with two shots each *starting* with the left target. You should be shifting your body weight (toward the next box) as the last target is shot. Explode to the right box, keeping the gun high on entering the box and fire two shots on the right target and then two on the left (working on shifting body weight again back toward the left box). Explode back to the left box keeping the gun high, and fire two shots on the left target and two on the right. Reload between boxes if necessary due to division capacity.

Critical Points: Remount (re-grip) the gun early and high when entering a position. Gun should be extended before you stop your body, not after. When possible, enter with the lead foot (Left if moving left, right if moving right). Stabilize the gun and press through the trigger when the sights settle (accept some wobble/movement).

Mental Cues: Actively visualize the entire drill.

Visual Cues: Keep the gun just below vision level until entering the box. Wait for the sights to settle before pressing the trigger.

Advanced Distance: N/A

Phase 3: Add two more boxes 5 yards uprange of the two initial boxes, which will allow you to practice moving uprange (start at the rear left box, move forward, right, rear, and left).

IDPA Option: Utilize cover garment, and set up magazines for slide lock reloads.

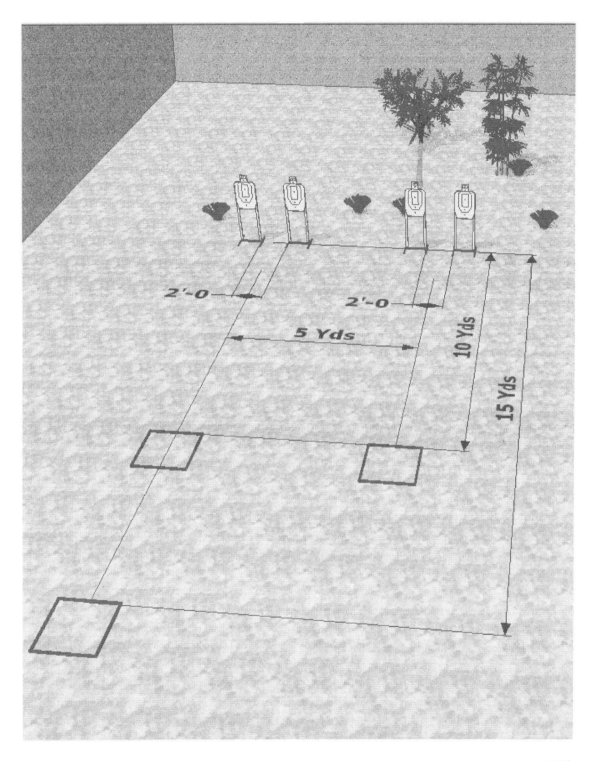

2'-0
2'-0
5 Yds
10 Yds
15 Yds

125

By: Mike Seeklander

Shooting and Moving, forward and backward

Rounds Per Repetition	12	Total Rounds	
			120
Total Repetitions		Accuracy and Time Goals	90% A's, no D's
	10		

Purpose: To learn how to correctly perform the firing cycle on the move, stabilizing the gun and calling good shots.

Start position: Holstered, hands relaxed at sides.

Target type and setup: 3 IPSC, set at 7-13 (see prop setup) yards with 1 yard between each target.

Prop setup: Set up with a center cone 10 yards away and centered on the middle target (we will remove this cone when set up). Place a cone at each number on an imaginary clock on the ground 3 yards from the center cone. (6 o'clock should be 13 yards from the target, and 12 should be 7 yards if set up correctly)   Remove the middle cone. You can also set this up without cones, by just marking spots on the ground.

Action/s: Starting at the 6 o'clock position (in front of the cone), on the timer, draw and fire 2 rounds on each target while moving forward, perform a speed (competition) reload and repeat moving to the rear.   That is one repetition. Call each shot. Force yourself to move at a speed that gets you to the cone you are moving toward. Practice the following directions each twice (forward and backward with a reload between): 6-12, 5-11, 7-1, 4-10, 8-2. When engaging targets shoot them in the order that you are moving when you are practicing on the angles.

Critical Points: Heel to toe and toe to heel movement, short steps. Stabilize the gun and press through the trigger when the sights settle (accept some wobble/movement). Scoring will be done by counting total points, as time is less relevant on this drill.

Mental Cues: Actively visualize the entire drill.

Visual Cues: We must have a very hard focus on the front sight, and should always know where the gun is aligned while moving. The shots should be going off and it is critical to call the shot when the sight or dot lifts.

Advanced Distance: N/A

Phase 3: N/A

IDPA Option: Utilize a cover garment, and perform slide lock reloads

Credit Goes To: Phil Strader, find Phil at: www.straightersolutions.com

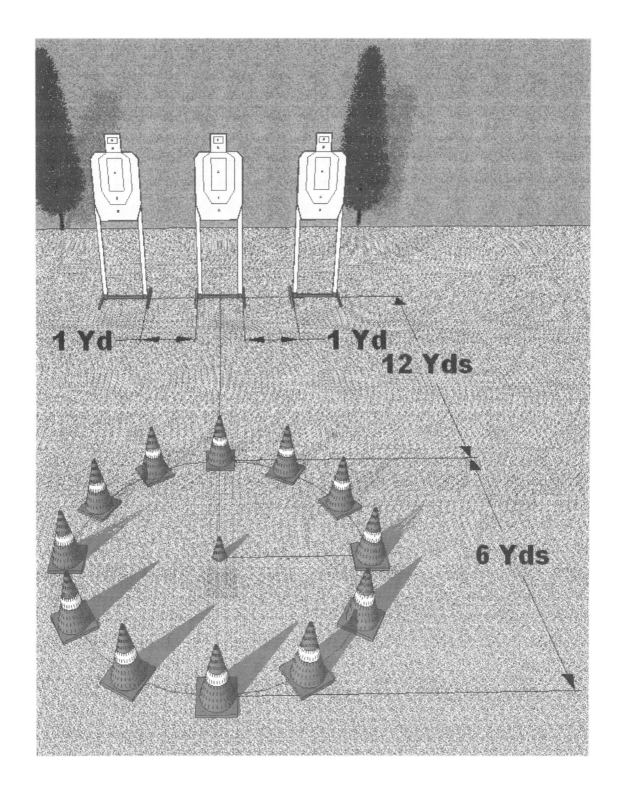

By: Mike Seeklander

Shooting and Moving, Multi-Directional

Rounds Per Repetition	18	Total Rounds	
			90
Total Repetitions	**5**	**Accuracy and Time Goals**	**90%** A's, no D's

Purpose: To work on multi-directional movement.

Start position: Holstered, hands relaxed at sides one yard behind either barrel.

Target type and setup: 3 IPSC set at 10 yards directly in front of the shooter, with 1 yard between them).

Prop setup: Two barrels (or something similar, set 10 (front edge) yards from the targets spaced one yard apart.

Action/s: Begin with 3 magazines of 10 rounds. On the timer beep, draw and fire 2 rounds on each target (L-R) while moving between the barrels (shooter will make a figure 8 sideways). Perform a speed or slidelock reload while continuing to move. Re-engage the targets again, reload, and re-engage again (for a total of 18 rounds).

Critical Points: Keep the weight low, and float the gun in front of the face, and watching the sights. Scoring will be done by counting total points, as time is less relevant on this drill.

Mental Cues: Actively visualize the entire drill.

Visual Cues: We must have a very hard focus on the front sight, and should always know where the gun is aligned while moving. The shots should be going off and it is critical to call the shot when the sight or dot lifts.

Advanced Distance- Increase distance to 15 yards

Phase 3: N/A

IDPA Option: Utilize a cover garment, perform slide lock reloads

Credit Goes To: Dave Paasch (former USSA Rangemaster)

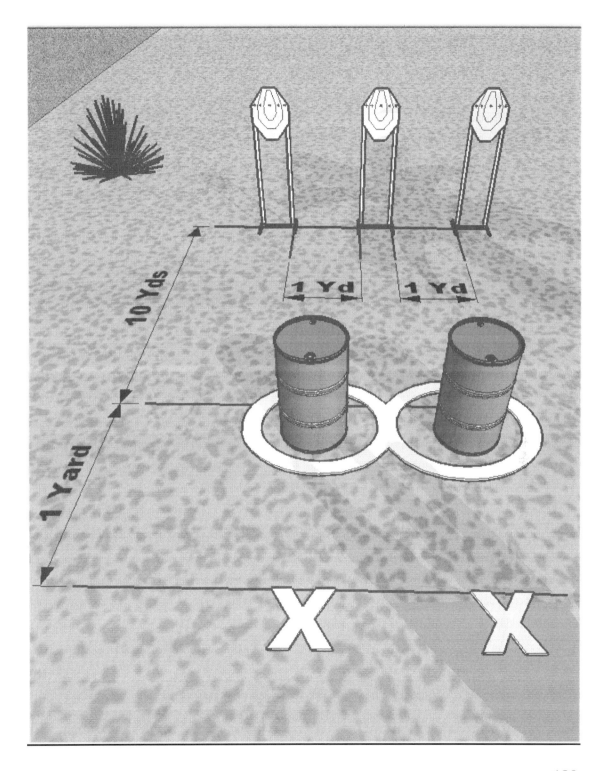

By: Mike Seeklander

Shooting and Moving, Aggressive Entry

Rounds Per Repetition	12	Total Rounds	
			60
Total Repetitions		**Accuracy and Time Goals**	90% A's, no D's
	5		

Purpose: To work on multi-directional movement.

Start position: Holstered, hands relaxed at sides standing behind barrel of choice.

Target type and setup: 4 IPSC targets, divided into two groups of two centered directly in front of the each of the barrels with 1 yard between them.

Prop setup: Two barrels or something similar set 10 yards (front edge) from the targets and spaced 6 yards apart.

Action/s: On the start signal, draw and explode to the opposite barrel, and fire two rounds on each target after braking and while moving around the front of the barrel (your shots will occur while you are moving around the front arc of the barrel and somewhat to the rear). Sprint to the next barrel, and repeat, and then back to the other barrel and repeat again for a total of 12 rounds. If necessary, reloads should occur between barrels.

Critical Points: Keep the gun high when sprinting. Remount at least two steps before the next position (as you are braking). While shooting, floating the gun in front of the face, and watching the sights. Scoring will be done by counting total points, as time is less relevant on this drill.

Visual Cues: We must have a very hard focus on the front sight, and should always know where the gun is aligned while moving. While the shots are going off it is critical to call the shot by watching the front sight or dot lift.

Mental Cues: Actively visualize the entire drill. Mental key is the hit on steel.

Advanced Distance: Increase distance to 15 yards

Phase 3: N/A

IDPA Option: Utilize cover garment.

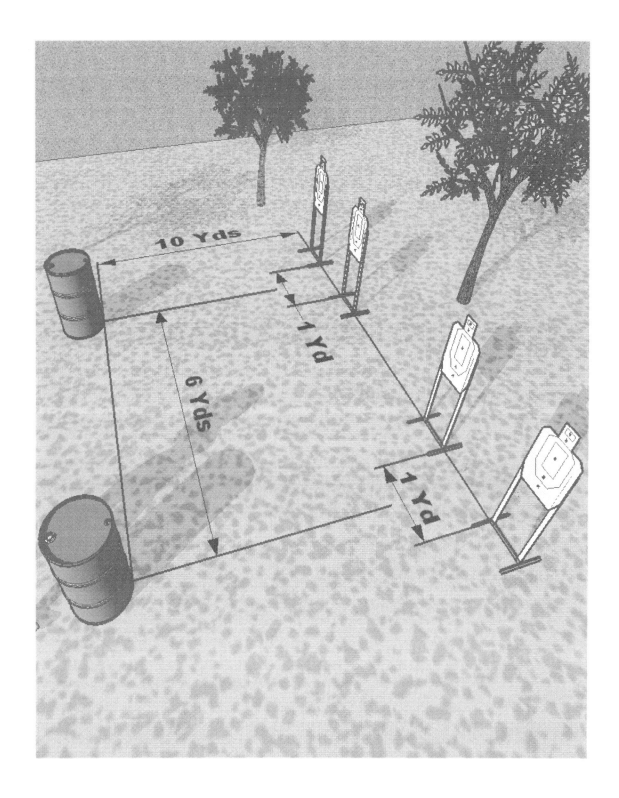

131

By: Mike Seeklander

Target Acquisition

Rounds Per Repetition	5	Total Rounds	
			50
Total Repetitions		**Accuracy and Time Goals**	**90%** A's, no D's
	10		

Purpose: To learn how to correctly perform the firing cycle during target acquisitions.

Start position: Holstered, hands relaxed at sides.

Target type and setup: 2 IPSC, one 8 inch plate, or small pepper popper (preferably resetting or non-falling for time's sake) with the plate/popper set as the center target at 10 yards directly in front of the shooter. The 2 IPSC targets should be 5 yards on either side of the steel target.

Prop setup: N/A.

Action/s: On the sound of the timer, draw and fire 1 round on the plate/popper and 2 on each target alternating which one is shot first (left or right). Repeat for a total of 10 repetitions.

Critical Points: Stopping and calling a good shot on the first steel target. Prep the trigger as the gun is driven to the next target and enters the target area (not before). Stopping or pausing the gun as much as needed to fire the shot. Drive the gun hard to the next target. Pay attention to the mechanics of the firing cycle during the shooting.

Mental Cues: Actively visualize the entire drill. Mental key is the hit on steel.

Visual Cues: Look at the spot we are driving the gun toward. When the front sight/dot touches the aiming area we should be verifying alignment and placement of the sights.

Advanced Distance: N/A

Phase 3: N/A

IDPA Option: Utilize a cover garment

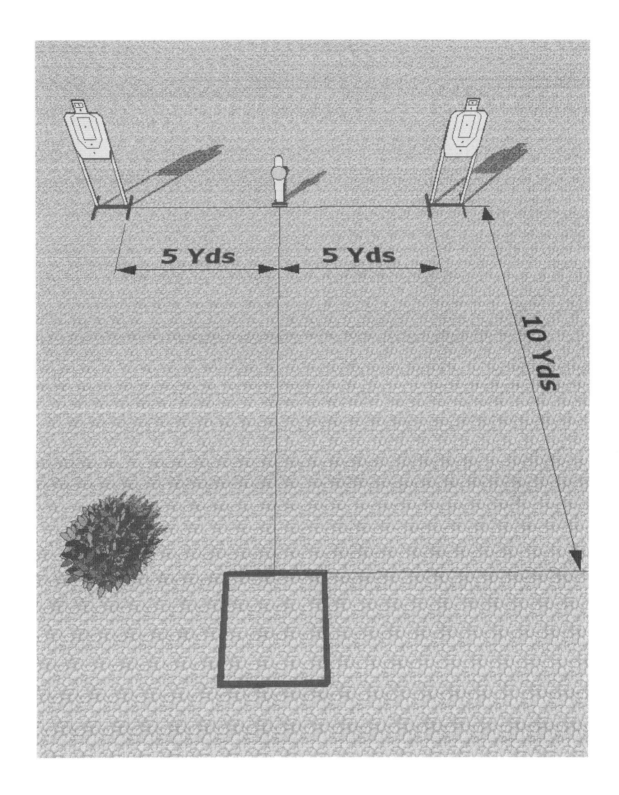

By: Mike Seeklander

One Shot X-Drill

Rounds Per Repetition	8	Total Rounds	
			48
Total Repetitions	6	**Accuracy and Time Goals**	**90%** A's, no D's

Purpose: Recognition of the correct sight picture (faster), and target acquisitions of varying size targets.

Start position: Holstered, hands relaxed at sides.

Target type and setup: 2 IPSC 5' high at the shoulder, 7 yards directly in front of the shooter 3 yards apart.

Prop setup: N/A.

Action/s: Draw and fire one round to each of these target areas and repeat the sequence (for a total of 8 rounds per repetition). Alternate your starting point and follow the sequences below (three of sequence 1, and three of sequence 2).

1. T1 body, T2 upper, T1 upper, T2 body
2. T1 upper, T2 body, T1, body, T2 upper

Critical Points: Seeing what you need to see to hit the A-zone shot on the two different target areas. The pace should be completely different between a body and headshot. Prep the trigger as the gun is driven to the next target and enters the target area (not before). Stopping or pausing the gun as much as needed to fire the shot. Drive the gun hard to the next target. Pay attention to the mechanics of the firing cycle during the shooting.

Mental Cues: Actively visualize the entire drill.

Visual Cues: Look at the spot we are driving the gun toward. When the front sight/dot touches the aiming area we should be verifying alignment and placement of the sights.

Advanced Distance: Increase distance to 10

Phase 3: Increase distance to 10 yards, or 12 yards if started at advanced distance

IDPA Option: Utilize a cover garment

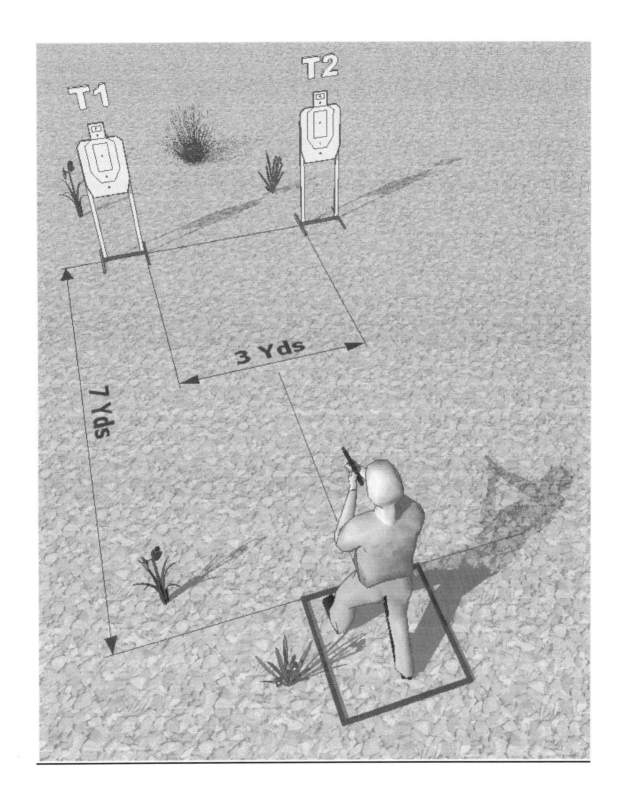

135

Two Shot X-Drill

Rounds Per Repetition	16	Total Rounds	
			80
Total Repetitions	**5**	Accuracy and Time Goals	**90%** A's, no D's

Purpose: To learn how to correctly perform the firing cycle during target acquisitions of varying size targets.

Start position: Facing up range, holstered, hands relaxed at sides.

Target type and setup: 2 IPSC 5' high at the shoulder, 7 yards directly in front of the shooter 2 yards apart.

Prop setup: N/A.

Action/s: On the sound of the timer turn, draw, and fire two rounds to:

> ➤ T1 upper, T2 body, T2 upper, T1 body

Reload, and repeat the sequence.

Critical Points: Seeing what you need to see to hit on the two different target areas. The pace should be completely different between the body and head shots. Prep the trigger as the gun is driven to the next target and enters the target area (not before), stopping or pausing the gun as much as needed to fire the shot. Drive the gun hard to the next target. Pay attention to the mechanics of the firing cycle during the shooting.

Mental Cues: Actively visualize the entire drill.

Visual Cues: Look at the spot we are driving the gun toward. When the front sight/dot touches the aiming area we should be verifying alignment and placement of the sights.

Advanced Distance: Increase distance to 9 yards

Phase 3: Increase distance to 10 yards, or 12 yards if started at advanced distance

IDPA Option: Utilize a cover garment, and set up magazines for slide lock reloads.

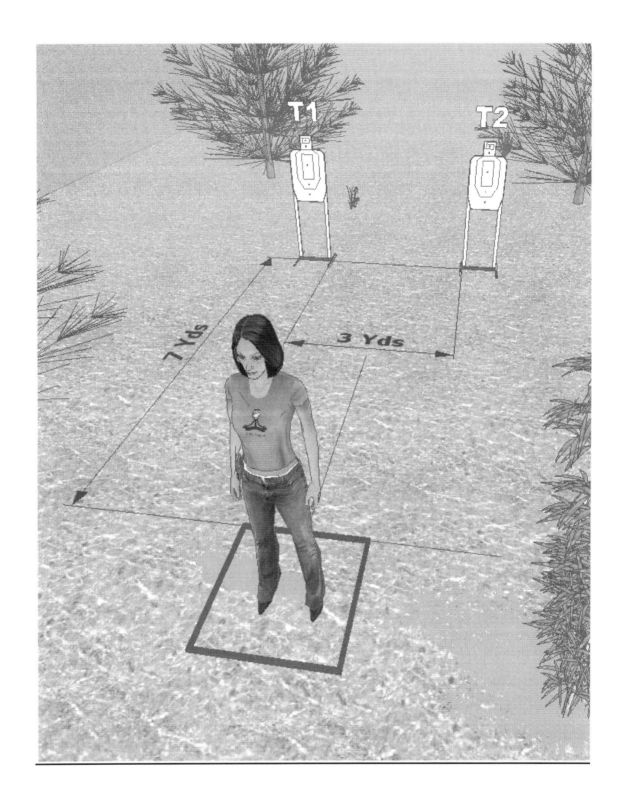

　　　　　　　　By: Mike Seeklander

Barricade X-Drill

Rounds Per Repetition	16	Total Rounds	
			80
Total Repetitions	5	Accuracy and Time Goals	90% A's, no D's

Purpose: To learn how to correctly perform the firing cycle during disadvantaged shooting positions, with varying size targets.

Start position: Hands on barricade, holstered.

Target type and setup: 2 IPSC 5' high at the shoulder, 7 yards directly in front of the shooter 1 yard apart.

Prop setup: One Bianchi type barricade (24-30 inches wide), set one yard in front of the shooting position (six yards away from the target).

Action/s: Start with the hands on X's on barricade, feet inside the barricade box or no wider than the barricade. *Right Handed shooter*- On the sound of the timer, draw and fire two rounds to:

> ➤ T2 upper, T1 body, T1 upper, T 2 body

Reload, and repeat the sequence on the other side starting on T2. Start on the opposite side and reverse the sequence if you are left-handed.

Critical Points: Seeing what you need to see to hit the A-zone shot on the two different target areas while leaning around the barricade. The pace should be completely different between a body and headshot. Prep the trigger as the gun is driven to the next target and enters the target area (not before). Stopping or pausing the gun as much as needed to fire the shot. Drive the gun hard to the next target. Pay attention to the mechanics of the firing cycle during the shooting.

Mental Cues: Actively visualize the entire drill.

Visual Cues: Look at the spot we are driving the gun toward. When the front sight/dot touches the aiming area we should be verifying alignment and placement of the sights.

Advanced Distance: Increase distance to 9 yards (target to barricade)

Phase 3: Increase distance to 10 yards (12 if starting at advanced distance)

IDPA Option: Utilize a cover garment and use the barricade for cover (follow IDPA rules), shoot in tactical order.

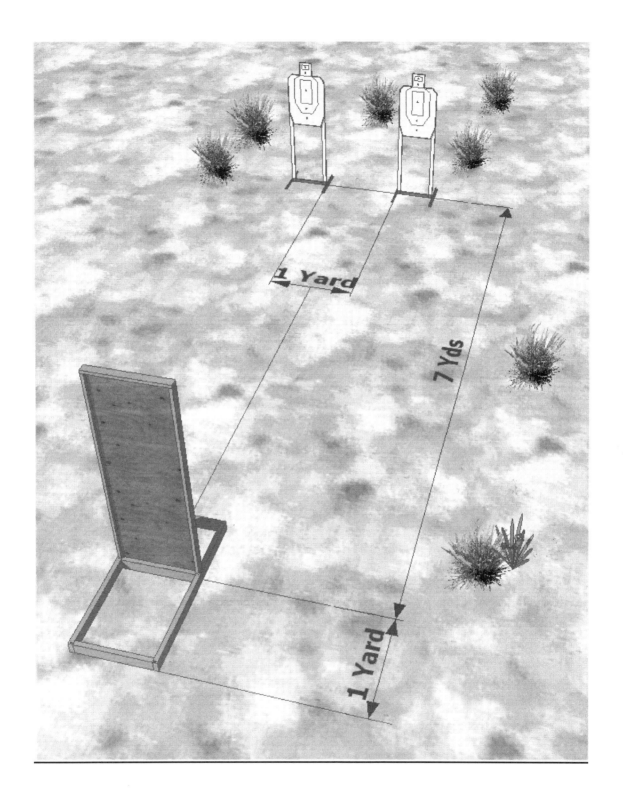

1 Yard

7 Yds

1 Yard

By: Mike Seeklander

Strong and Weak Hand X-Drill

Rounds Per Repetition	16	Total Rounds	
			80
Total Repetitions		Accuracy and Time Goals	90% A's, no D's
	5		

Purpose: To learn how to correctly perform the firing cycle during target acquisitions of varying size targets using only the strong and support hands.

Start position: Holstered, hands relaxed at sides.

Target type and setup: 2 IPSC 5' high at the shoulder, 5 yards directly in front of the shooter 2 yards apart.

Prop setup: N/A.

Action/s: Starting with hands relaxed at sides, draw and fire two rounds **strong hand** only to:

> T2 body, T1 upper, T2 upper, T1body

Reload, transfer to weak hand and fire two rounds to

> T1 body, T2 upper, T1 upper, T2 body.

Critical Points: Prepping the trigger and seeing the sights is critical with the strong and support hand. Maintain a locked wrist and strong grip while firing the gun with one hand. Reload/transfer should be in front of the face and the finger MUST be out of the trigger.

Mental Cues: Actively visualize the entire drill.

Visual Cues: Look at the spot we are driving the gun toward. When the front sight/dot touches the aiming area we should be verifying alignment and placement of the sights.

Advanced Distance: Increase distance to 7 yards

Phase 3: Increase distance to 7 yards, or 10 if started at advance distance

IDPA Option: Set up magazines for a slide lock reload, and utilize a concealment garment

Credit Goes To: N/A

By: Mike Seeklander

Multi-Port Drill

Rounds Per Repetition	16	Total Rounds	
			80
Total Repetitions		**Accuracy and Time Goals**	**90%** A's, no D's
	5		

Purpose: To learn how to move quickly to different shooting ports and to improve the ability to execute the firing cycle from those positions.

Start position: Holstered, hands relaxed at sides.

Target type and setup: 2 IPSC, set at 10 yards directly in front of the shooter 3 yards apart and 5 feet high at the shoulder.

Prop setup: A standard IPSC target stapled upside down so that the bottom of the target is the height of your shoulder (this will be different for each of you). Cut the A zone out and head off the target. You now have 4 different shooting positions: A. left side, B. middle port (medium squatting), C. right side, and D. below the bottom of the target (low squatting/kneeling). This prop should be placed directly in front of you far enough away so that it is a couple inches away from the muzzle of your gun when it is fully extended.

Action/s: Starting directly behind the prop, engage each target with two rounds shooting the left target first and then right in each position in this order A, B, C, and D. Repeat the drill shooting the right target first and then the left in this order C, B, A, and D. Reload as needed between ports.

Critical Points: Moving your body and gun together so that you maintain a solid upper body triangle. The lowest position should be engaged from a low squatting position if possible rather than a kneeling position if you are flexible enough. Maintain the same grip tension throughout the drill. DO NOT retract and extend the gun between ports.

Mental Cues: Actively visualize the entire drill.

Visual Cues: Wait for the sights to be in the target area before shooting. Be patient on the sights when in low or off balance positions.

Advanced Distance: Increase distance to 15 yards (move prop too).

Phase 3: N/A

IDPA Option: Utilize a cover garment, and set up magazines for slide lock reloads

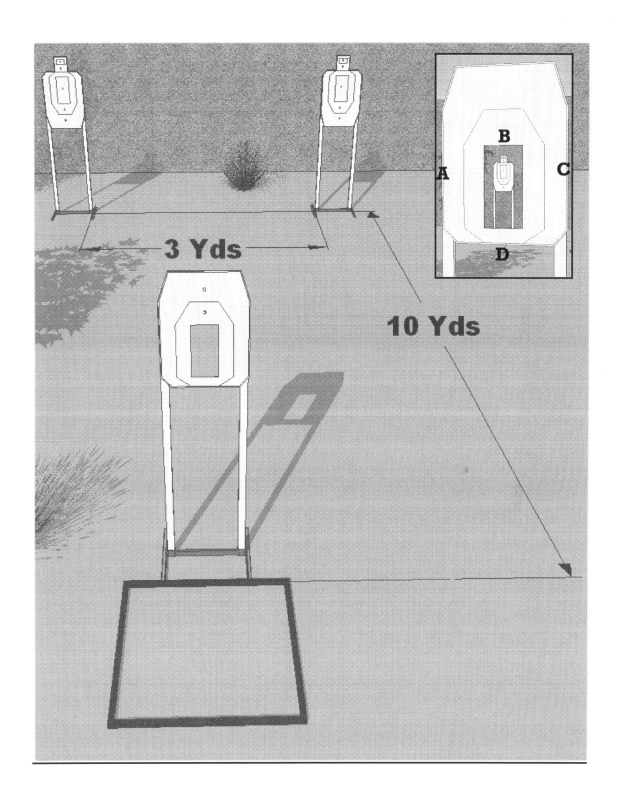

By: Mike Seeklander

Multi-Position Drill

Rounds Per Repetition	8	Total Rounds	
			40
Total Repetitions		**Accuracy and Time Goals**	**90%** A's, no D's
	5		

Purpose: Note: This drill is physical, be sure to warm up and stretch first. To learn how to move quickly to different positions and to improve the ability to execute the firing cycle from those positions.

Start position: Holstered, hands relaxed at sides.

Target type and setup: 1 IPSC, set at 15 yards directly in front of the shooter.

Prop setup: N/A.

Action/s: On the timer, draw and drop to a kneeling position (one knee down), and fire two shots to the body A zone, return to standing position and fire two shots to the upper A zone, drop down to the prone position and fire two shots to the body A zone, return to standing and fire two shots to the upper A zone.

Critical Points: Wait for the sights to settle between positions. Move quickly, and ensure finger is out of the trigger.

Mental Cues: Actively visualize the entire drill. See yourself moving explosively.

Visual Cues: Wait for the sights to be in the target area before shooting. Be patient on the sights when in different positions.

Advanced Distance: Increase distance to 20 yards

Phase 3: Increase distance to 20 yards (or 25 if using advanced)

IDPA Option: Utilize a cover garment

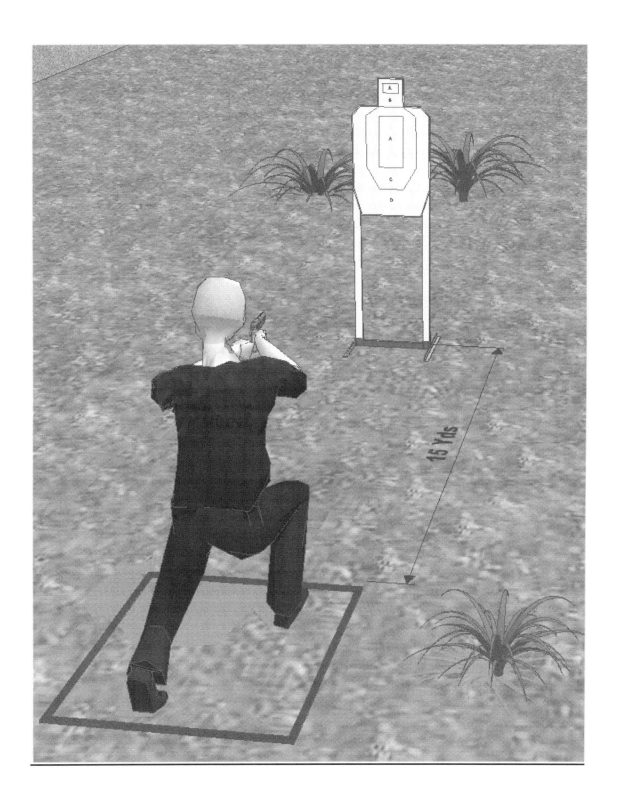

15 Yds

145

By: Mike Seeklander

Long Range Challenge

Rounds Per Repetition	6	Total Rounds	
			60
Total Repetitions		**Accuracy and Time Goals**	**90%** A's, no D's
	10		

Purpose: The fundamentals of shooting and hitting at long distance.

Start position: Holstered, hands relaxed at sides.

Target type and setup: Three Standard IPSC set up at 30 yards, 1 yard apart, 5 feet high at the shoulder.

Prop setup: N/A.

Action/s: On the timer beep, draw and fire 2 shots to the A zone of three targets at a pace that will GUARANTEE hits. Learn the pace you can fire and hit the A/C zone.

Critical Points: Sight alignment, Grip pressure on the gun, continual movement of the trigger.

Visual Cues: Patiently wait for the sights to settle and align.

Mental Cues: Actively visualize the entire drill.

Phase 2: Increase distance to 40 yards.

Phase 3: Increase distance to 50 yards.

IDPA Option: Utilize a cover garment

146

1 Yard

1 Yard

30 Yds

147

By: Mike Seeklander

Multi-Hardcover Target Drill

Rounds Per Repetition	8	Total Rounds	
			40
Total Repetitions	5	**Accuracy and Time Goals**	**90%** A's, no D's

Purpose: To learn the proper index points on hard cover targets, and the speed at which they can be shot.

Start position: Holstered, hands relaxed at sides.

Target type and setup: 4 hardcover IPSC (left diagonal, tiger, half hard cover, and right diagonal), set at 12 yards directly in front of the shooter.

Prop setup: N/A.

Action/s: On the timer, draw and fire two shots to the center of the available high score target area on each target. Each target will have a different index point.

Critical Points: Wait for the sights to settle between positions. Move quickly, and ensure finger is out of the trigger.

Mental Cues: Actively visualize the proper index points in this drill.

Visual Cues: Look for the index points on the target, and drive the front sight/dot to those points.

Advanced Distance: Increase distance to 15 yards

Phase 3: Increase distance to 20 yards

IDPA Option: Utilize a cover garment

Copyright 2010 Shooting-Performance   By: Mike Seeklander

Summary: Lets summarize the *Live Fire Training Module*:

☐ The skills trained in the live fire training sessions will specifically improve your ability to shoot better (apply the firing cycle skills of sight, trigger, and grip management). There are certain components of each drill that will teach you how to improve key areas in the firing cycle in different circumstances.

☐ There are three key timeframes during live fire training and there are certain things that are important during each of these timeframes:
  o Pre Session- this is the area directly before you train.
    ▪ Go through your mental toughness routine.
    ▪ Review and prepare for the training session by reviewing last sessions notes.
    ▪ Set up targets and props for the upcoming drills in the training session.
  o During Session- this is the timeframe when you will actually be training.
    ▪ Actively visualize each repetition before you do it. ("See yourself do it, then do it")
    ▪ Video if a camera is available.
    ▪ Document your times and all data during the drill. (This will include scoring hits after the specific drill is done)
  o Post Session- This is the timeframe directly after the session is over.
    ▪ Document any last minute notes about your session, be complete as possible.
    ▪ Review how the session went, and pre-fill any key data on your next log sheet to remind you of what you may need to address or focus on in your next training session.

☐ The live fire drill sheets have details that will have to be followed when performing them, including the number of repetitions you will do. Make sure to follow them completely, and read them before you set up and start. Once you get used to doing them, they will become easier to set up and execute. Your live fire drills are broken down into two types:
  o Micro Drills- these are small drills that separate one or two components of a drill and allow you to focus on one or two portions of the technique.
  o Macro Drills- these are larger, more complicated drills that put multiple skills together. They are designed to allow you to put the techniques together, as well as to work on the mental side of visualization.

☐ You will follow a three-day per week live fire schedule that may be modified into less than three days per week if necessary. Less than two days per week is not recommended. Sessions that are not completed should not be skipped, but done during the next training session. Your three sessions will be broken down by skill set:

- o *Fundamental Skills*- this session focuses on fundamental shooting skill sets.
- o *Movement Skills*- this session focuses on movement.
- o *Specialty Skills*- this session focuses on specialty skills.

☐ There are three separate training phases, increasing in difficulty and varying in length. As you gain more skill, the drills will become harder and more complicated.

☐ You will take one full week off from shooting between phases, to decompress and refresh.

☐ The drill sheets contain all the information necessary to complete each drill.

By: Mike Seeklander

CHAPTER FIVE
Mental
Toughness Routine

"All great performances come from the mind"

By: Mike Seeklander

The topics I will cover in this chapter:

1. *Skills trained in the mental toughness program*
2. *Mental Toughness vs. Mental Connection*
3. *The Mental Toughness routine (breathing exercises, success statement, self image booster, visualizations)*
4. *Active vs. Passive visualization*

Mental Toughness Training

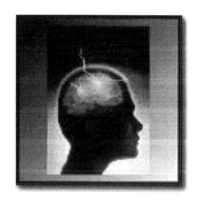

<u>**Skills Trained**</u> -The mental toughness routine will be done each time you train (as well as portions during other times) and will increase your ability to perform on demand under pressure. Performing well after some practice at *your* range while you are alone is not a problem for most of us, but when we enter "game day", things usually change. Most mental preparation material out there is great, but difficult to apply. I have taken the time to distill the best mental training tips I have found and incorporated them into this short mental toughness routine. The following material will educate you about some key mental concepts and my beliefs about them. I want to educate you about these principles before I give you the routine. Following this information will be your routine. It will help guarantee your success, so pay close attention and do the routine when assigned.

<u>**General Discussion/Introduction: "Theory of a Miss"**</u> - Some time ago, while trying to figure out why I was making mistakes, while knowingly making them (observing the mistake happen yet not being able to stop it), I developed a theory called "theory of a miss" Theory of a miss is a defining observation that describes the mental system breakdown causing the common "miss" under stressful situations (matches). The term "miss" can certainly be used interchangeably with any mistake

made during a match or real world event (game day), and is not meant to be a limiting term. Most shooters (athletes) understand the physical dynamics behind a mistake under stress, but few know the mental factors involved that lead to the mistake or how to correct them. This section will cover that material, and may very well be the key to flawless performance on demand.

The Root of all Mistakes - The word mistake implies that a wrong decision has been made, which in practical shooting is incorrect. The "miss" (a mistake) in our sport happens at high speed, within the sub-conscious level of thought processes (usually), and can't be controlled (most of the time), even though you may know you are making the error. Why can't it be controlled? Likely, because you have trained yourselves to make the error. When training repetitions are repeated multiple times a "program" is written into your subconscious to control those physical skills in the future. The root of this uncontrollable mistake is the subconscious mind and how it works. Let's take a closer look at the subconscious and conscious mind:

Conscious and Subconscious, *A Comparison* - Comparing the subconscious mind and the conscious mind is like comparing an adult to a child. The infant, prior to the age of about two, does not have the ability to make decisions between right or wrong. After the age of two, and increasing in age, children and adults have the ability to make decisions based on information and can determine between right and wrong in general terms. You process information based on beliefs and stored information that you deem necessary. Now let's compare that to an infant, somewhere around the age of one. At that age, the infant has the ability to process information, but for many different reasons cannot assess whether the information is right or wrong. The infant simply processes the information and records it for later use in life. The infant does not have the ability to screen that information and store the good stuff and reject the bad like we do as adults. When comparing the

155

By: Mike Seeklander

conscious and subconscious portions of the brain, the conscious brain is like the adult. It has the ability to reason, reject incorrect information. The subconscious portion of the brain is like the infant, unable to reason or reject information. It just stores information and stores it well. Each and every small detail is stored because it has such a capacity for knowledge (similar to an infant's brain that is stimulated more when it encounters more information). The conscious portion of the brain accomplishes analytical or logical thought processes. The subconscious portion of the brain accomplishes automated and automatic processes. The conscious portion of the brain triggers the subconscious portion to engage during times of high anxiety, stress, and believe it or not during times of zero anxiety, while accomplishing mundane tasks. Think about it, when you drove home from work the last time, did you consciously have to think about turning on your blinker, or even hitting the brake? Probably not, as these actions are all handled with relative ease by the subconscious mind after being prompted by the conscious decision making process (see stop sign, decision to stop, hit the brake).

As I was working with a shooting athlete the other day at the range, I observed something that I've seen time and time again, and have even observed myself doing. I had this athlete working on a drill that involved managing his trigger and sights on two different target types, forcing him to utilize varying trigger pulls in one string of fire. I had set up two targets at about 5 yards from the athlete and spread about 2 yards apart. In between those two targets, about 12 yards away, I had placed a small mini pepper popper. The drill was simple: draw and fire two shots on the left paper target (with a certain type of trigger pull), one shot on the steel (with another type of trigger pull), and then two more shots on the other paper target, perform a reload, and repeat that array of targets with the same number of shots. This particular athlete was going to be repeating the drill approximately 10 times. At about the fifth or sixth time, I stopped him and pointed out the fact that out of those six runs, he had fired two shots on the paper, one miss on the steel, two shots on the other paper all while missing the steel target each time. Sometimes he proceeded to make up his miss on the steel, and at others, he failed to make up the miss on the steel. When asked, the athlete had no problem telling my why he had missed the steel target repeatedly.

His mistake was a simple timing error coupled with poor sight alignment. While the athlete could answer the question of "why he was missing the piece of steel," one thing that did not stand out to him was the fact that over those six repetitions he had already began to program his subconscious mind to perform a mistake. He knew why he was missing, but did not know how to fix it. Think about it for a second, every time he fired at that piece of steel, he fired at it with either misaligned sights or a trigger pull that was incorrect. So visually, in his eyes, he must have seen something incorrect, and that visual input was transmitted through his optic nerves to his brain, which prompted him to do something, i.e. pull the trigger. So he sees the sights visually which keys his brain to continue to manipulate the trigger to the rear causing the gun to go off. The problem is that the shot was an incorrect shot.

This means that he was training the subconscious area of his brain to manipulate the trigger with the wrong visual stimulus. His subconscious mind did not understand that the sight picture and timing of the shot was wrong, although consciously he knew he was making a mistake. The problem is that now his subconscious mind had six repetitions of this improper technique written into it. When I asked him why he was missing the steel he replied, "Because the front sight is nowhere near the center of it!" "Well," I said to him, "if you have repeated that same sight picture six times in a row, or let's say for the sake of discussion a 100 times in a row during a given training session, then what are you training your subconscious mind to do?" He answered, "I guess I'm training myself to miss".

By: Mike Seeklander

You see, even a simple drill in which we're firing at targets or a piece of steel can cause us to write the wrong subconscious program into our computer (our brain). Once this program has been written it's at <u>least</u> double the work to correct and rewrite it correctly. The act of repeating a skill allows us to improve that skill through a process called myelination.[5] This process coats the nerve pathways with a substance called myelin, which is a fatty substance that helps the nerve transmission travel faster. The more a skill is practiced, the faster that nerve transmission is, hence the improvement that comes from repetitions of any skill. The big problem is that once a nerve becomes coated with myelin, it cannot be "unmylenated", and the only way to correct a bad habit due to improper myelination of the wrong set of nerve paths is to write (myelinate) a new and stronger path. So, if the initial skill took five thousand repetitions to write (myelinate), then the new one will take at least that many, and then some so that it becomes the primary path that is selected by stimulus to run a skill.

Now this athlete went through multiple repetitions of missing the steel, and as I have discussed, this trained him to perform that way under stress (miss!). Another problem is that if he missed a piece of steel during training on a regular basis, what do you think that did to his self-image? Nothing good, I can tell you that. It could create a negative self-image and belief that he cannot hit a piece of steel at that distance of that size in a match.

<u>Subconscious Skills</u>. This is the area that one great author calls the "skills factory" and rightly so. The subconscious portion of the mind is where key components of a specific skill set are stored for use under stress, and also during common repetitive tasks. The entire premise behind the Shooting-Performance company and website is: "Correct Design and Perfect Execution." This refers to designing a training

---

[5] Daniel Coyle, <u>The Talent Code</u> (New York: Bantam Dell, 2009).

program correctly (so you train the right subconscious skills), and then executing those training sessions perfectly (so you ingrain them properly). Ingraining skills happens at the subconscious level, and is necessary in order for you to perform complex movements at extremely fast speeds. When you build subconscious skills you are writing "skill programs." When an athlete is performing, they will be running skill programs that were written during their training sessions. These small programs will run all or portions of a skill from start to finish as dictated by a conscious thought (information processing). Most people think that the best performances are all subconscious, but this is untrue during events that cannot be memorized or trained repetitively. The truth is that the decisive thought process and sub-conscious must be in concert. The real key is that the sub-conscious programs must be written into the brain (like a computer hard drive) properly or when ran, they will perform the wrong processes, even if you consciously know they are wrong. Skill programs are written by repetition, and don't forget that the repetition is not judged by the subconscious mind as correct or incorrect, it is simply recorded.

<u>Self Image.</u> Your self-image is who you believe you are. Your self-image dictates your confidence (or lack thereof) in your ability to act a certain way or do certain things. It is built as a result of your entire life experiences, and it is one of the most powerful things you can manipulate in your training that will impact your performances in a positive manner. Your self-image will cause you to believe in yourself or not, and this creates an emotional state that is either positive or negative. While the actual beliefs in your self-image are important, I don't believe that they alone affect your performance. Think about it for a second; what you believe doesn't literally affect the outcome of a performance. Now, the *emotions* you experience because of your beliefs <u>do</u> affect the outcome, because your emotional state will actually change the physical state the body is in. I will expand more on self-image in the next section where we discuss emotional control.

Emotional State. Your "emotional state" is the mental condition you are in when performing. It is the often-overlooked piece of the puzzle that truly paints the picture of whether a performance was true and repeatable, or just luck. Those top athletes, who perform well, in what some call the zone, do it while they are in a positive emotional state and feel in control. I have found elements of this theory in almost every single mental training resource I have ever read. Eliminating negative emotional triggers and creating a positive emotional state are largely the goal of mental training, and what I believe to be the true secret to performing well. I pay particular attention to my emotional state when training (control zones) and performing. Don't confuse nervousness with negativity, as many athletes perform exceptionally well when they are nervous. It is very possible to program the brain and convince the self-image to believe that your best performances are when you are nervous, while at the same time feeling in control. Emotional triggers can be either positive or negative and will result in a corresponding emotional state. Common negative emotional triggers are as follows:

> *First Experience Memories*. These are memories created during your first experience(s) of a particular sport or event. Most athletes competing in practical shooting for the first time at match feel an incredible amount of stress and anxiety. This occurs because of a lack of self-confidence in their ability. In our first experiences we will often see things that seem to be repeatable and "easy", but they are far from that. How many of you remember trying to go as fast as your local guy who was at the A class level in USPSA and then failing miserably when doing so? This is also the case for those in law enforcement and the military who have never shot before and have watched most of the shooting they have ever seen on T.V. They watch actors do things with guns that are unlikely and pretty much wrong and then

160

try to repeat this skill. This memory or experience is so strong sometimes that it is carried with us during years of competing. Most shooting athletes that I work with have been trying to go too fast for their entire shooting career and have never really learned how to perform "in control." This lack of control leads to a dead end road that is unavoidable. One of the steps outlined below (acceptance) is often the hardest step in fixing this error. Most shooters just don't want to slow down and train themselves to do what they have to do to succeed. This trigger can be overcome by experience and skill development. Positive self-talk can aid in reducing this effect on performance.

> **Primers**. I call anything that reminds you of something that causes you stress a "primer." It is a primer to a negative emotional state. For you competitors, an example might be seeing the top shooters in their sponsor shirts. Why would this "prime" you to be in a negative emotional state? Because you normally don't see those shooters when you are shooting your club match. They only show up at the big matches, which your brain automatically labels as important. Anytime the stakes get high (important), your brain tells your body to prepare for battle and you tend to feel more stress, even though the skills you need to perform are the exact same skills you use in practice and at your club match. For you military guys and gals, a negative primer for you might be arriving at the rifle or pistol range if you have had a negative experience there before. Your brain remembers the stress you felt while trying to qualify and attaches that to the location you experienced the stress. If you have negative self-talk going on while you experience these primers, things get worse.

> **Self Image**. Your own self-image is also a huge emotional trigger that can have catastrophic effects on your performance. "Getting over" ourselves is

By: Mike Seeklander

sometimes the hardest thing to do. A poor self-image is largely a result of previous failures, or more so the lack of self-forgiveness. Athletes should hold themselves accountable for their mistakes and take corrective action via hard work, not self-punishment. When you punish yourself internally and hold yourself to impossibly high standards of perfection, you set yourself up for failure. Self-image is the key to unlocking full potential, and without a strong self-image athletes will do well but will never do their best. Keys to building a positive self-image are positive visualizations, self-talk, and most importantly, self-forgiveness. Mistakes happen, get over yourself and find solutions to the errors. Look at a mistake as an opportunity to learn "why" something happened and improve.

> *Fear of Failure*. This is probably the most common emotional trigger and it is linked directly to self-image. The fear of failure resides deep in most competitive athletes and stems from a mentality that failure is not an option. If this were correct, then no professional athletes would exist. They would all commit suicide and sport would disappear. We develop a fear of failure because we have all failed at one time or another and it is disturbing. Realistically, a fear of failure can be tamed by changing the way an athlete thinks. Failure to accomplish a certain goal or level can be looked at as something so positive and powerful that, if used correctly, will drive an athlete to certain success. Here is the key: failure must be understood as the single propellant that has driven all great successes to the levels they reached. This author has yet to find a person, company, or story of a great success without repeated failures first, sometimes hundreds of failures! The key is to change the way you think, and continue to move forward. Why do something if it is going to be easy? This manual exists because this sport is hard to master.

> *Laziness*. Laziness may not seem like a common emotional trigger but it is. Laziness in a training program results in lack of self-confidence. Those that do the work deserve to reap the rewards, and when an athlete slacks on their training they cause internal doubt to start growing inside the recesses of their mind. This lack of confidence may not be apparent when they are competing in an environment where they feel they are the superior athlete, but will surely surface when the going gets tough. The only cure to this emotional trigger is the work. When an athlete does their homework and has put in the time, they will have an incredible amount of confidence when competing.

> *Trying too hard*. Yes, believe it or not, trying (usually to go fast) stimulates thought patterns that can cause negative emotional states. Think of it this way, have you ever tried to walk? Seriously, go ahead and stand up and *try* to walk. You will stumble or feel awkward. When you walk, you just do. When you place too much emphasis on *trying* to do something, you set yourself up for failure. Trying to go fast is the exact opposite of what you should be doing. Train the mechanics so thoroughly that the speed just comes, and forget trying. *Do* instead.

Learning Emotional Control - In order to rebuild emotional control and place yourself in a positive emotional control zone there are several key steps that we can follow. Remember, learning emotional control is a key part of the process of learning how to do anything in control. Here are some things that you can do to rebuild or learn how to place yourself in a positive emotional control zone:

> *Do the Work*. Nothing puts us in a better emotional state than solid preparation. The only person you cannot lie to is you. If you have done your homework and have prepared well and worked hard, that is the first

163

step in placing yourself in a positive emotional state and boosting your self-image. This entire book is a about designing your training sessions so they will allow you to excel, so you can check this box if you are reading, learning, and acting on the guidance you have read.

> *Acceptance.* Accept that there may be some setbacks when trying to un-train certain negative processes. Just taking the time to slow down and learning to perform techniques in control is incredibly difficult. I spend most of my time on drills that twist my brain in knots because I mix easy and hard shooting skills together, and then I force myself to slow down enough to perform the technique I am working on correctly. Another thing you need to do is remove the do or die attitude from performances. Practical shooting is an incredibly rewarding sport and really means a lot to some athletes, but it should not be so important that it causes a negative emotional response because of a fear of failure. If you are training for combative purposes, you may actually have a do or die performance, but if you allow it to dominate your mind you will not perform at your best. If you have done the work (step one), then don't worry; your performance will match your preparation.

> *Forgiveness.* During the process of moving into the elite performance levels, you will undoubtedly fall off the track several times. As stated in a previous section, failure drives all great successes. This author has personally experienced and witnessed the greatest athletes in history making critical mistakes in the heat of competition. If it can happen to them, it can certainly happen to anyone!

> *Baby Steps.* Take one step at a time when rebuilding emotional control. Start by fixing practice routines so that they build proper skills and thus confidence. Move to applying those skills in practice stages and mini tests, always striving for the emotional state of being in control even

while under extreme stress. Further that by applying those learned skills and emotional zones at local or small matches, or during small training exercises (for the combative arena) and then graduate up the chain all the way through to game day. The point is, use the crawl, walk, run principle.

➢ ***Positive Self-Talk***. One of the best ways to retrain your brain and turn a negative primer into a positive one is to change your self-talk. It is believed that we have tens of thousands of conversations of self-talk each day. Imagine if you used these self-talk conversations for positive purposes. I will cover this in detail in the actionable steps to building mental strength.

➢ ***Expanding your Control Zones***.   For competitive athletes I teach three levels of emotional control called "zones." I think the principle would also apply to those of you getting ready for a fight, but these zones were primarily designed to put a name on the different performance zones we can find ourselves in when shooting in the competitive world. Emotional control zones are relevant and connected to the speeds that you shoot, but speed itself does not dictate what control zone you are in.   Actually the opposite is true.   Ultimately, the level of control you feel when performing at that particular speed dictates the control zone you are in. When you are training your physical skills, you should be focusing on expanding the control zone you want to be in during practical shooting competitions, which is Zone 2. Each zone has a physical speed that is associated with it, as well as emotional characteristics. The chart on the following page will show how each zone has key physical and emotional characteristics.

By: Mike Seeklander

The Control Zone Chart on the next page that shows the differences between zones 1, 2, and 3.

Control Zone	Physical Characteristics	Emotional Characteristics
Zone 1	This zone is slow fire. It is the zone that you would find yourself in if you competed in bullseye type matches. The only emphasis in this zone is accuracy. You RARELY ever enter Zone 1 in practical shooting.	There is no pressure in this zone so emotional state is completely relaxed. Heart rate and anxiety should be very controlled (low) in this control zone.
Zone 2 **The optimum zone!**	This zone is the perfect performance-shooting zone if speed and accuracy are both important, and falls somewhere midway between Zones 1 and 3 in terms of physical speed. It is the widest zone (if the three were divided up), and the more you expand it the better you get. You are always trying to expand this zone of control deeper into zone 1 (accuracy) and zone 3 (pure speed). The emphasis in this zone is equally balanced between speed and accuracy.	There is pressure in this zone, yet the predominant feeling is control. Heart rate and anxiety may be higher than when in zone 1, but are at a level that does not interfere with your performance. Emotionally, this is actually the "zone" that is referenced in many books and videos. You may not have perfect recollection of what happens during this zone, because they are largely subconscious (yet not totally).
Zone 3	This zone is the redline zone. You should almost never end up in this zone yet most shooters end up here when they push themselves over the edge. There is nothing to gain in this zone and everything to lose. You do not have the ability to control your physical skills at this speed.	You are performing outside of the confines of what you can control, and this is very risky. You are most likely in a negative emotional state in this zone, and probably feel out of control. You may not have recollection of what happens in this zone, mainly because you are not paying attention to what is happening.

Building Conscious Control (memory) - Conscious control in practical shooting sports consists of priming the brain to make correct decisions at speed (meaning in a split-second). Without this ability your conscious mind cannot make decisions like it needs to and will get "lost" during performances. The conscious mind and the subconscious skill programs are connected when you perform a group of processes at high speeds (i.e. shoot a stage or get into a gunfight). The conscious mind (memory and decision making ability), guides the subconscious to run subconscious skill programs when needed. The best way to give the conscious mind a clear pathway to follow is to use solid visualization techniques. Visualization is the act of seeing yourself do something in your mind, without physically doing it. It is very similar to daydreaming, yet with a purpose. Proper visualization is one of the keys to every great athlete's success. If you are an athlete reading this book, hoping to perform your best at a match, then understand this: The key to running a successful mental program while shooting a match without making mistakes is proper visualization.

Mental toughness - Mental toughness is a term I have heard throughout the years as I have competed against the best shooters on the circuit. You also hear this term on a regular basis on sports shows when announcers are talking about the ability of some of the great players to perform when the pressure is overwhelming. Mental toughness is primarily made up of confidence, and is critical if you want to meet your goals. Whether you just want to win your division at the sectional championship in your state, or a world championship, you will need to be mentally tough to succeed. Any one of us can perform well when we are at the practice range; the trick is to keep those skills consistent with the high-pressure arena you will be in at a large match. You will develop mental toughness in this program by doing a mental training routine each time you train that includes things such as perfect execution of the drills (to develop confidence in your skills), visualizing yourself

167

succeeding (to develop confidence in your abilities under pressure), and focusing on positive images and using positive words (to put and keep yourself in a positive mental state).

<u>Mental connection</u> - The term "mental connection" means that you have to commit to connecting mentally with every skill you train in practice thus allowing that same connection at a match. One of the biggest mistakes I see people make when training is that they go through the motions during their training drills, instead of mentally connecting with each and every repetition. To get mentally connected in this program, you will perform active visualization exercises during your training sessions and at matches. There are keynotes on each training drill that will remind you of the visual and mental cues that are important during that skill development. Pay attention and use them and this will maximize your learning experience.

<u>Your Mental Training Routine</u>[67] - The following routine can be done as one short 10-15 minute routine, or can be done in pieces. I want you to do this routine before your live fire training sessions and dry fire training sessions. In addition, you will also use the passive visualization techniques during other periods of time on most days (really any time you want, the more the better). One key to doing this mental routine before and during your training sessions is that it will increase your ability to use those same mental techniques at a match. It amazes me how many competitors expect themselves to be able to use visualization techniques to shoot a stage better at a major match, yet do not train with visualization while at their home range during their training sessions. Failure to use the same mental techniques in training will greatly reduce their effectiveness at the event (match). In this program you will be live or dry fire training five or more times per week, and you will do your

----

[6] Jason Selk, <u>10-Minute Toughness</u> (New York: McGraw-Hill, 2004).

[7] Lanny Basham, <u>With Winning in Mind</u> (Wilsonville: BookPartners, Inc. , n.d.).

mental routine then, so you will be working these skills five times per week, which will really help with your mental game.

There are four main components to your mental routine, they are: the *focus breath*, the *performance statement*, the *self-image booster*, and *visualization techniques* (active and passive). Each of these components will be written onto 3X5 cards that you place in your range bag, or training areas as a reminder to go through your mental routine each time you train. I recommend getting some 3X5 cards ready now, as you will be using them soon.

Lets break each component down:

1. ***Focus Breath***- The type of breathing I am talking about here is designed to help you control your heart rate during stress. I originally learned "combat breathing" from a martial art instructor who used the technique to focus his mind and lower his heart rate before and during sparring matches. I have since found some ways to improve the technique that I originally learned. Lowering your heart rate is important, as it will lower your arousal level to the point where you will find the most mental and physical performance benefits. Normally, arousal level and heart rate will increase when you feel stress because of a preconceived level of importance placed on a particular event or action. For example, if I told you to shoot and hit a head shot on a standard IPSC target at 5 yards, most of you could do it easily and your heart rate would normally stay pretty close to your resting heart rate levels. If however, I took your 5-year-old child or significant other and had them stand very close to the target you were shooting at, do you think your heart rate would increase? Of course it would, even though the shot was exactly the same. Because of the potential risk to your child you would place much more importance on that shot for fear of hitting the

By: Mike Seeklander

wrong target. When you feel stress, your heart rate increases and this can impede performance. An increased heart rate is not always a bad thing though, and some heart rate increase is important to perform well, but too much of an increase causes all sorts of problems when you are trying to perform. Visual skills, fine motor skills, decisive skills, etc. have all been shown to decrease when you increase your heart rate to more than about 200% of your resting heart rate. The chart below shows how the heart rate affects performance. The numbers on the left are the heart rate. Resting heart rate is probably around 50-70 beats per minute, and as you can see too low for good performance. The performance zone is about 110 up to 140 or so, with anything above 150 where skills start to seriously degrade. Heart rates above 170 cause irrational behavior and deterioration of fine and complex motor skills.

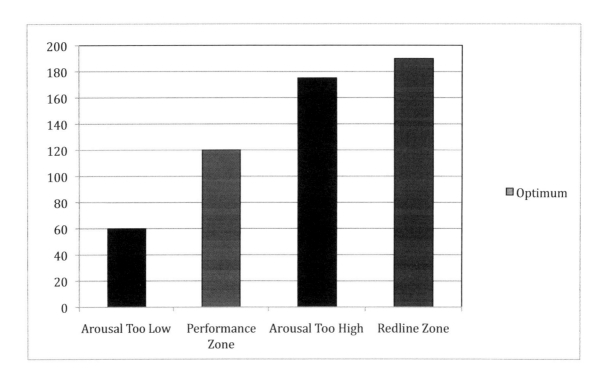

The following breathing exercise will lower your heart rate significantly when you do it, allowing you to stay in your performance zone. A great side benefit to these exercises is better oxygenization of the blood, which improves your reaction time and visual skills as these systems all rely on oxygen in the blood. The more you practice this technique, the better it will work when you need to call upon it under stressful situations. A side note is that if you reverse this process (quick shallow breathing through the mouth), you can have the opposite effect of increasing arousal and heart rate levels. Here is how it works:

➤ *Breathe through the nose.* Breathing through the nose is key to lowering your heart rate. For several reasons, when you breathe through the nose, you automatically begin to lower your heart rate because your body is designed to breathe through the nasal cavity versus the mouth. Mouth breathing causes a variety of stress related responses because during a fight or flight response, humans tend to breathe through the mouth to get more oxygen and activate their survival instincts that are designed to increase gross motor function.

➤ *Breathe deep from the diaphragm.* Diaphragm breathing requires very deep breaths, which allows the diaphragm to expand. Sometimes this is called "belly breathing" because when you do it right your belly tends to expand rather than your chest expanding or rising, which is what most of us do when we breathe. The truth is that most of us breathe wrong. To increase your success in breathing with the diaphragm, you will use a technique that forces you to breathe deeply and fill the lower lobes of the lungs with oxygen. To do this, you will do the following:

  o *Inhale for a count of 5-6 seconds (through the nose)*
  o *Hold the breath for a count of 2 seconds*
  o *Exhale for a count of 5-6 seconds (through the nose)*

By: Mike Seeklander

o *Note: Make sure to let your belly expand when you do this as this helps you breathe with your diaphragm (hence the term belly breathing)*

This long 13-15 second breath will force you to breathe deep if you follow it correctly. This will lower your heart rate and increase your fine and complex motor functions. It will also oxygenate your blood and increase your information processing and visual skills. Use this breathing technique during training right before you do your mental workout as well as any other time you are feeling stressed out. Use it often in practice as well as club level matches to improve your ability to lower your heart rate. I often combine this breathing technique with a physical trigger (I grip my handgun in the holster if I have it on), visualizing myself relaxed and in control. By doing this repetitively, I have created a reflexive action when I grip my handgun (don't remove it from the holster), and get a relaxing mental response when I am stressed out. Another example might be going through this focus breath while stretching during a pre-stage routine. If trained enough times, the act of stretching would in itself begin to lower the heart rate back to the performance zone. Once again, you will need to master and practice this during training repetitively in order for it to work at a big match.

Your task: Go ahead and write the following on the top of one of your 3X5 cards: *Focus Breath 6-2-6*

2. ***Performance Statement***- Your *performance statement* is a short, powerful statement that will keep you in the present and remind you of what you have to do to succeed. More specifically, your *performance statement* is a simple and concrete statement that will help you control your thoughts under pressure, which will help keep you in a positive emotional control zone. I recommend developing one or two for use during key times, but you could certainly develop

more.   If you are a multi-sport athlete, consider developing one for each shooting sport you do. You can even create one for each individual stage of the sport you do if desired. For example, the Steel Challenge (world speed shooting championship) is a specialized match that requires you to do different, yet key things on each stage in order to perform well. For that match you might have one general *performance statement* that you can use anytime, and some key *performance statements* for certain stages that require something special. I would also recommend developing them for stages or events that you might have had a problem with in the past, to give you something to think about before you start to have negative thoughts creep into your mind.   We all think during high-pressure events, but the best shooting athletes know that they have to decide *what* to think about rather than letting their minds wander. The key is to develop a statement that will contain the key elements of what you need to do (processes) in order to execute the skill well. Even in the most complex shooting events, there are not really many complicated skills we need to do to perform well. One of my personal success statements is "grip the gun, see the sights, relax and flow with it." This may seem overly simple, but if simplified, what else do I need to do to hit the shot? You might say, pull the trigger correctly, or keep the gun steady, etc., but I already know I will do those things automatically because of my training. To start the action and set me up for success mentally, I use this short statement to simplify and keep my mind focused. I know that if I see the sights after getting the gun on target, I will hit the shot. I also know that gripping the gun right will assist with fast follow up shots and will keep me shooting at the pace I need to be. I don't have to worry so much about where to pressure the gun in my grip, because I have trained that to the subconscious level, just like pulling the trigger. When my subconscious mind sees the sight

173

By: Mike Seeklander

picture, it recognizes it as correct at the distance I am shooting and the gun will go off automatically.

Your performance statement should be used regularly in training, and use it before and during every drill you do between repetitions. When you use your statement try to visualize yourself executing what you need to do to be successful.

To write your *performance statement*, do the following:

> Ask yourself what the two or three most important things you will need to do to perform well. Think about what a good instructor or coach may tell you before you shoot the stage or event. Take a piece of paper and write those two or three things down. If you have more than three, go ahead and list them all. Now take that list and form those things into a statement that will simply remind you what to focus on under pressure. Your statement should be short and to the point, with no more than two to three key action sentences.

Once developed, you will use your success statement(s) during training and high-pressure events before you perform on a stage or training drill. For now, go ahead and write it down on a 3 x 5 index card, right below where you wrote your focus breath details. If you have multiple statements for different stages or sports, keep them on separate cards. Title your card: "*Performance Statement*". During training take your index card out and remind yourself of what your statement is, and take a moment to visualize yourself doing the things in your statement. Remember the mental connection you are trying to create during training. Each time you do a drill, recite your *performance statement*. I also recommend you begin to develop a physical trigger at the same time you use your statement. Like I said before, my physical trigger is

174

gripping my handgun in the holster when I think or read my statement. Pick something subtle that you know you will be able to do during a high-pressure event. Repeat this over and over again to create a physical trigger that will help you regain or maintain focus when you are stressed out.

3. **Self Image Booster**- Your *self-image booster* is a future statement outlining something you are going to do. One thing that has been proven over and over again is that when you tell yourself something, your mind will try to find a way to accommodate you. That is why the big rule in sports psychology is to stay positive in thought and statement at all times. Negative thoughts will eventually turn into negative actions. Your self-image booster will be a short paragraph written in first person that will have one to three sentences (or a few more) that describes the you that will allow you to meet your goal. I can't tell you how much research and information there is out there in the sports psychology world that validates the theory that you have to believe in your ability before you can ever actually accomplish something. Developing your self-image is one of the keys to your success. This self-image booster is simply a tool to help it along. I know some of you might be thinking that this is something you might not take seriously, but I strongly encourage you to do this step. Now, full disclosure about self-image boosting tricks, they will not work unless you have done your part of the bargain. Read this statement: "I work harder than anyone on the shooting circuit and have a relentless focus on preparing thoroughly. I am the best competitor on the shooting circuit." Good Statement right? This would actually be a pretty good self-image booster. Will it work though? Lets say that I repeat that statement over and over again every day for one year. Will that, in itself, boost my skill to the ability where I am actually the best competitor on the shooting circuit? No, unfortunately not. A self-image booster must be accompanied by the work (the training) in order for it to produce the desired

175

By: Mike Seeklander

result. Internally knowing the work has not been done will cause insecurity and a lack of confidence. You can lie to anyone in the world but yourself, and if you have not done the preparation, then boosting your self-image via false means will not create the desired result.

How do you know if you are doing enough preparation? Sometimes it's hard to be certain, but ask yourself: was anything else you could do to better prepare yourself for the last event you competed in? If you can say yes, there was something else you could have done, ask yourself one more question: Was your best competitor doing those things to prepare? He or she probably was. Get to work!

Developing your statement is very simple:
1. *Write your statement in first person.*
2. *List your strengths and traits that show you have what it takes to meet the goal.*
3. *List what you want to accomplish.* First of all, you will have to accept that you will be writing a statement that has not occurred yet, and it may seem exaggerated. Remember you are boosting your self-image toward where you want to go, if you were already there you would not need this book. I have seen this several ways and one way is to write this sentence, stating that you are the winner or current champion of whatever it is you are trying to win. Another way is to list this statement more general in nature, and instead of writing that you are the current champion of whatever, you simply write how good you are, which will obviously facilitate winning whatever you try to win. I personally like to use the second approach, because it is more believable for me to write where my skill level is because it is

something that I can control, versus that I am a winner of a certain match (my mind keys in on this and rejects it). Either way, here are examples of each:

a. *I am a tenacious, dedicated, and relentlessly hard working competitor who is a threat to anyone I compete against because of my focus on preparation. I am unstoppable in competition and I am the 2012 IDPA National Champion.*

b. *I am a tenacious, dedicated, and relentlessly hard working competitor who is a threat to anyone I compete against because of my focus on preparation. I am the fastest and most accurate shooter in the United States and am unstoppable in competition.*

Another option is to repeat the end statement (what you want to accomplish) twice by starting with it and finishing it. Example:

> *I am unstoppable in competition and I am the 2012 IDPA National Champion. I am a tenacious, dedicated, and relentlessly hard working competitor who is a threat to anyone I compete against. Because of my focus on preparation I am unbeatable. I am unstoppable in competition and am the 2012 IDPA National Champion.*

One thing that this statement has to have to work is reality. It has to be REAL. As I have said before, you can not lie to yourself and write a long, complex self-image booster that is not believable to you because you know you are not doing the work, and expect it to do what it is designed to do. Once you have written your statement, take your 3 x 5 cards that have your *performance statement/s* written them and write your *self-image booster* on

177

it. The key is to read this statement each time you train or do anything that relates to your goal. More often, the better. You might be inclined to skip reading it or feel foolish doing this, but I promise you this will affect your outcome. Reading a short paragraph will take you less than 10 seconds, what have you got to lose?

4. ***Visualization Techniques***- Visualization is mental imagery. Seeing yourself doing something before you do it is an incredibly powerful tool, and is one that I see neglected by many shooters out there. I have surveyed each class with a question during a mental lecture I teach for the last several years, and have found that almost all of the students I have fail to use visualization to the level that the top shooters use it. Does this tell you something? There are two types of visualization, *active* and *passive* and they both have a different purpose and timeframe for use. Key Details:

> ➤ ***Active***- Active visualization is mental imagery that should be used when you are actually doing the activities of your sport. Whether you are training or competing, active visualization should be used to increase your mental connection to what you are doing. Every one of the professional shooters I surveyed for this book use visualization when they are competing. They know (as do I) that visualizing helps build a mental map of the stages they are shooting. They have two primary reasons for doing this. First, they use it to help them remember and follow through better with their plan on the stage. Secondly, they visualize themselves performing well which increases their performance on the stage, even though they have never shot it before. The brain will follow a visualized "mapped" route much more efficiently than an unplanned (un-mapped) process. There are a

couple matches out there that are memory matches and have stages that are always the same. These matches can be shot from memory and visualization is primarily used in these types of matches to boost successful execution of the stage (the better you see yourself shoot the stage, the better you will actually shoot it). IDPA and USPSA (IPSC outside the U.S.) matches normally have stages that the competitor has never shot before, and thus could not have practiced. These matches require visualization to memorize the stage sequence as well as to increase successful execution of the stage. To learn how to use visualization correctly, you will use it during your training drills, as well as in matches. Key concepts:

- o *Use the first person view.* This means that you should visualize as if your eyes are cameras and you are watching the action through these cameras.
- o *Use all the senses.* When you visualize, you should visualize more than just visual input. Visualize information such as touch, sound, smell, and yourself experiencing emotion while performing the actions.
- o *Visualize at the correct speed.* This is critical, and is something that can really hurt you if you do it wrong. Your subconscious mind does not know the difference between what happens in visualization and reality. Therefore, if you see yourself doing something at the wrong speed, you will likely perform the action at the speed you saw yourself doing it. Make sure you visualize yourself doing the action the same speed that you really want to do it. This is critical in sports like shooting

179

because we have perform at a speed that will allow us to maximize the hits in order to succeed. Another problem might occur if you visualize yourself shooting faster than you should on hard targets, which will likely cause you to do that during the performance, resulting in poor hits. Pay attention to the speed you see yourself performing the actions on the stage, as your mind will execute whatever you visualize.

- o *See the skill from start to finish.* If you are visualizing a stage at a match, or a drill in training, see yourself doing it from start to finish. This will increase the reality of your visualizations, and the learning experience it will create.

- o *Pay attention to the details.* Similar to the speed concept above, remember that you really need to pay attention to what you visualize. Your brain will learn and repeat what you program into it. Make sure you visualize all details correctly.

Okay now you understand the key concepts, lets talk about how you will use active visualization in this program:

- o *Actively visualize each drill repetition before you do it.* This is for both dry fire practice and live fire drills. This might be new to you and you will have to make yourself do it at first. Write it on your training logs as a reminder if you need to. Make absolutely sure you visualize all drills before you do them. If you make a mistake during a drill, stop and take the time to visualize yourself doing that particular action right several times before you do the next drill. I always tell my students to "See yourself do it, then do it". Your training sessions should look like this: visualize it, do it, visualize it, do it, etc.

o *Actively visualize each stage before you shoot it.* I have a rule that requires ten or more visualizations of a stage before I am ready to shoot it, and sometimes even then I am not ready. This is applicable in all matches. In club level matches I find that shooters tend to skip this or pay less attention to doing it correctly, because the match is less important to them. This is a huge mistake since practicing your visualization techniques at the club match level will help you improve your visualization and execution ability at larger matches. My rule is that you should be able to face away from the stage you are shooting and visualize yourself shooting the entire stage, seeing each target array as it appears (if it is a hard cover target or no-shoot, or whatever), and each position as it actually is. Obviously, the bigger the stage, the more times you might have to visualize the targets and positions before you get them memorized. If you have gotten lost or forgotten targets during stages before, then the act of planning and then repeatedly visualizing your plan will fix this. Some of you may have to repeat the visualization more than others, but just remember that you are not ready until you can run the stage from start to finish in your mind and see everything in detail as it actually is.

➢ *Passive*- Passive visualization is more of a self-image booster than a direct memory or performance tool like active visualization. Your use of passive visualization will be different than active in that you can do passive visualization anytime, anywhere. In this program you will do a short passive visualization exercise each time before you train.

By: Mike Seeklander

Passive visualization is best done in a combination of first person and second person views. First person is like viewing what the action would look like through your eyes. Second person would be watching yourself perform from the perspective of having someone else take a video of you. I recommend using both angles in whatever manner that seems to come natural to you. I want you to create your own *success visualization* (like a video in your mind), and here are the steps to doing it:

- *First, create a "success video" of yourself.* It will be composed of clips of three key things:
  - You training and preparing
  - You shooting well at a recent event
  - You shooting well at the next match you will compete in.

  Each clip will be 30-60 seconds in length, and you should see yourself in a positive manner, performing exceptionally well during all three clips. For example, during your first clip (training and preparing), see yourself shooting the drills in this program extremely well and working very hard at them. Your second clip should come from your memory of a stage or several stages at recent matches that you did great on. Your third clip will have to be imagined, but try to see everything about the upcoming match in total detail, going great. See yourself as the superstar that you are! You will run your self-image video each time you train, right before you start. I visualize myself in training first (working real hard and shooting well), which sets the stage for the next video I play of me doing well at a match, I then end with a short mental video of me doing well in the next event I am training for. The total time spent doing this can be well less than 3-5 minutes, but if you have longer feel free to really create a powerful video and mentally view it several times.

o *Secondly, feel free to use passive visualization when you are not actively practicing or competing.* I recommend running your success video before bed each night as well as any other time you can (the more you run it, the more you will boost your self-image).

o *Now, write a couple bullet points about each clip* in your success video on the same 3X5 card that has your *focus breath*, *performance statement*, and *self-image booster* on it. You might want to write this on the back, so you can be relatively detailed about it.

o *Finally, as an event approaches, increase your passive visualization sessions.* Remember, the brain will remember what you visualize, so make sure all visualizations are positive and success oriented. The experience should be an enjoyable one.

Summary - You should have developed a performance statement, self-image booster, and short three-clip success video. They, along with a quick reminder about your focus breath should be written on a 3X5 card. I recommend duplicating a few of these cards, and placing them in your other training areas, and one in your car in case you forget one. Place one in your dry fire area too. When you find it you

183

will use it to go through your mental routine, and use the mental tools during your training session. You will be well on your way to some serious mental toughness.

Summary: Lets summarize the Mental Toughness Routine. You will:

☐ Use a special breathing technique to lower your heart rate and arousal state, increasing your fine and complex motor skills:
- o Each time you train, before you begin you will go through at least one repetition of the 6 in/ 2 hold / 6 out breath, through the nose.
- o Each time you feel stress or increased heart rate or arousal state at high-pressure events. This will likely be before each stage you shoot at a major match.
- o Any other time you want to lower your heart rate and increase the mental connection.

☐ Create a performance statement that will give you something simple and concrete to think about during high pressure events:
- o Read or say it before repetitions during training to increase the effectiveness of it at major events. Co-develop a physical trigger such as gripping your gun in the holster while you use your success statement to increase its effectiveness.
- o Use it anytime you feel negative thoughts coming into your mind. Repeat it as many times as necessary to keep yourself calm and focused.

☐ Create a self-image booster that will be composed of two or more sentences that remind you of where you are going. This self-image booster will be read before each of your training sessions, and anytime you come across the 3 x 5 card you have left in key areas of work (dry fire area, reloading area, etc.):
- o Read the statement and follow it with your passive visualization success video. Try to see yourself in a positive emotionally controlled state anytime you read your statement and go through your success video.

☐ Use Active and Passive visualization to increase your memory performance skills and self-image.
- o Use active visualizations any time you train and during all events to increase your ability to execute drills and stages better. Make sure to train the ability to see yourself do something then do it by using this technique in training as well as during matches.
- o Use passive visualizations each time you read your self-image booster by running your success video.
- o Increase your use of passive visualization immediately before an event. Visualize your success video each night before bed and the first thing in the morning for two weeks before a major event.

CHAPTER SIX
Physical Fitness

"Physical fitness is the great equalizer"

By: Mike Seeklander

The topics I will cover in this chapter:

1. *General concepts*
2. *Physical fitness basics (strength training, cardiovascular training, plyometric training, flexibility training)*
3. *Analyzing your needs*
4. *Building a program to meet your needs*
5. *Common mistakes made by shooters in their fitness programs*
6. *Recommended programs*

General Concepts - This program is designed to increase your ability to perform well in competitive shooting events. One of the things that I want you to incorporate is physical fitness in your training program. I believe strongly in the benefits of physical fitness for competitive athletes, and I guarantee that you will increase your chances of success if you are physically fit. While I say this, I do not have the space in this book to write a complete physical fitness program for you and would not be able to do so because each of you have individual unique needs. Because fitness is so important, I will speak about some general concepts and then give you some recommendations that are simple and easy to follow.

Physical Fitness Basics - In this section I will discuss some of the basic elements of physical fitness. I will attempt to utilize this space and your attention span to teach you about the elements of physical fitness that are important to your shooting goals. I do strongly recommend that you seek other books and resources on improving your physical fitness to the highest levels possible. Physical fitness is an incredibly important concept in any area if you want to perform on demand at the highest levels.

Physical Fitness 101 (for shooters) -

➢ *Strength Training:*

    o <u>Purpose</u>. Strength training consists of exercise/s that increase muscular strength. Increased strength will increase the amount of power a muscle can generate; therefore improving an athlete's ability to contract muscles explosively. This is important in the practical shooting sports because we have to move explosively from position to position, as well as get our bodies into and out of positions quickly. The higher our strength to weight ratio, the easier it will be for our muscles to move our bodies quickly.

    o <u>Information</u>. The programs recommended in this manual all include strength-training programs that are focused on increasing muscular development. Each offers a unique series of exercises that will train every major muscle group in the body. Excessive strength training during the active season utilizing heavy resistance (weights) may result in a lack of flexibility and tighter movement patterns. These are not necessarily a concern if a proper program is selected, as it will include exercises that increase flexibility and movement patterns. Lower body and core (midsection) strength will produce the best results in relation to movement through a stage. Building strength in these areas is a key that should be focused on. Ensure that lower body (leg) workouts are done early in the week so that match performance is not affected on a weekend. Leg workouts incorporating explosive movements are stressful and may cause muscular fatigue and soreness.

        By: Mike Seeklander

➢ *Cardiovascular Training:*

    o <u>Purpose.</u> Cardiovascular training consists of training the heart and lungs to work more efficiently.

    o <u>Information.</u> A good indication of general fitness is the body's ability to pump and utilize newly oxygenated blood through its system. Athletes will benefit by having a higher general stress tolerance, lower heart rate and blood pressure, more efficient fat burning processes, and better overall recovery after working hard on a stage. Cardiovascular exercises such as running, that mimic movements in practical shooting are the first choice when choosing what exercises to perform (if the athlete does not follow a recommended program). HIIT (High Intensity Interval Training) will serve the practical shooter best, as this type of cardio exercise will prepare the cardiovascular system to deal with the elevated heart rate associated with stressful endeavors. Competing will cause the heart rate to increase, and any exercise that elevates the heart rate to the upper end of its maximum will condition it to better deal with these stressors.

➢ *Plyometric Training:*

    o <u>Purpose.</u> Plyometrics may also be called jump training, and will train the neuromuscular system to explode (fast twitch muscle fibers) more efficiently. [8](Dintiman) Athletes should focus on this type of training (with caution due to the high potential for injury if done improperly) to increase their ability to move quickly and explosively through a stage.

    o <u>Information.</u> Both programs recommended in this program will incorporate plyometrics in their routines.

---

[8]George Dintiman, <u>Sports Speed</u> (Champaign: Human Kinetics, 2003).

➤ *Flexibility Training:*

  o <u>Purpose.</u>   Flexibility training consists of stretching the muscles to elongate them and allow for a greater range of motion. Muscles with an increased range of motion will allow an athlete to perform better when entering and exiting positions that require flexibility (low and abnormal positions).

  o <u>Information.</u>   Good flexibility will serve as one of the key factors in preventing injuries during explosive movement found within the practical shooting sports. The less an athlete is injured, the more he/she can train and improve technique and skills.

Analyzing your needs.   Analyzing your needs is a key step in deciding what physical fitness elements you will want to focus the most on during your training. You don't want to waste your time doing physical fitness related activities that are of no use to you. Think about it for a second, an Olympic shotgun shooter will have much different physical fitness needs, than someone who competes in a sport like practical shooting which requires flexibility and explosive movement. Even though there are physical fitness components that all of us will need, your individual goal(s) will dictate which ones you need the most. Do nothing of which is of no use. Your time is the most valuable thing you have. For those of you that are not doing a physical fitness program of any type, analysis of what you need may indicate you need a bit of everything. How do we analyze what physical fitness elements are important to us? Well once again, we have to go back to our goal and look at the elements within that goal. If you are a competitive athlete, who shoots practical type shooting competitions that require you to run and shoot and enter positions that require flexibility and explosive movement, then obviously you will have different needs than someone who is developing a physical fitness program for a more

189

defensive oriented use of a firearm. The good news is that even a generalized fitness program will greatly benefit most shooters who are not in good shape.

Although I recommend following a couple programs unless you have enough experience to design your own program, here is how you might analyze your individual needs for a self designed fitness program. I will break it down step by step:

1. **Document your needs (skills/movements).** With your goal in mind, right down all of the physical movement/ skills you use to meet your goal. Don't leave anything out! If you may have to run, then write down the word "run". If you may have to squat or kneel, then write down "squat" or "kneel", etc. Your list may look something like this:

   a. Grip/hold a handgun
   b. Run in any direction
   c. Kneel down
   d. Jump
   e. Stand for long periods
   f. Balance on something
   g. Squat down
   h. Push off the ground with one hand
   i. Pivot quickly in any direction

2. **Prioritize your needs.** Once you have written down all of the physical skills you use to meet your goal, then it is a good idea to prioritize those individual skills so you know which ones are used more often than others. Prioritizing these skills will allow us to focus our physical fitness-training program on the skills that we use the most. Obviously, we want a physical fitness program that is very

broad in scope; one that will cover and train all of the aspects that we will need to be physically fit enough to accomplish our goal. The danger is if we fail to train these physical fitness elements to the level we need to train them, then when it's time to perform on demand, we will be lacking in those areas.

3. **Select a program or elements for each need**. Step three is to take your prioritized list of skills and translate them into a physical fitness-training regimen. This means, for instance that if you prioritize your list and running was a skill that was near the top of the list, then obviously your physical fitness-training program should include elements of running. If you take the time to objectively analyze your prioritized list and the details within each of those skills, you should be able to select exercises that train those elements.

Building a program to meet your needs.   Now you have done the analysis on your needs, based on your goal. The next step is to build a physical fitness-training program that will meet those needs. This is where things can get a little bit complicated if you have no background and experience developing a physical fitness type program. I strongly recommend that you seek out an experienced trainer who can help build a program for you. A second option may be for you to select the programs that I have recommended and go through them in their entirety. After you have done this, you will have a very strong physical base allowing you to modify the programs as necessary to meet your specific goals.

Common mistakes made by shooters in their fitness program.   I now want to take a moment and discuss the common mistakes I see made by most shooters in their physical fitness training programs. I have observed numerous problems with

By: Mike Seeklander

physical fitness programs designed to improve fitness for shooting, and have made some big mistakes myself. Here are a few of the problems I have found:

➢ **_Low Strength to Weight Ratio_** - Strength training is a necessary method of training if you want to develop that explosive strength allowing you to move very quickly. Too many people have the misconception that strength (weight) training will quickly lead to bulky muscles and increased weight. This could not be further from the truth. In reality the problems with too much body weight often lies in the fact that most people carry much more fat than they should. Weight training will build lean muscle mass, and help burn the fat and at the same time increase strength to weight ratios. While I do not believe that excessive weight training is the key for movement in our sport, doing enough to build a good strength base will have very positive effects on your results. First, increasing your lean muscle mass will help burn more fat, even when you are not exercising (and remember most of us carry too much fat). Secondly, remember that strength is a necessary part of the movement equation. Having strong muscles that can explode quickly is necessary if you want to be able to explode from position to position, or move from a low to high position quickly. In theory, too much strength training could lead to over development of the muscle fibers and increased body weight, but this would be exceedingly rare. The last of your worries will be building too much muscle. For those that are training for an athletic event such as practical shooting and even those training for combative purposes, movement and explosive movement is a key concept that they need to be able to do well. Hit the weights and make sure to include some explosive movement (plyometrics) training in your program, you will not be sorry you did.

➢ **_Too little cardiovascular training_** - Cardiovascular fitness is one of the most important elements of fitness relating to shooting goals. From the bull's-eye shooter who stands and fires slowly at the target to the combative warrior who needs to use his shooting skills to save his life, cardiovascular fitness is an area that benefits us all. This is an area that I find many shooters lacking in. It is common to see athletes run through stages and at the end of the stage, observe them breathing extremely hard and sweating profusely. Cardiovascular fitness is an area, if trained to the highest levels, which will allow an athlete to perform at his or her best for numerous reasons. I have actually tracked my own heart rate during stages at a practical match and know for a fact that my heart rate reaches certain levels pre-stage, during stage and post-stage. When my cardiovascular fitness levels are at the highest, I perform at my best. If I can keep my heart rate under control or perform the techniques that I've trained with a lower heart rate then I have a much better chance at performing those techniques very well. It is clearly documented that as the heart rate increases beyond a certain level, skill normally decreases. Keeping the heart rate lower will have an obvious impact on skill performance. Cardiovascular fitness has an effect on our overall fitness and health, and should be treated as one of your priority elements when you build your program.

Note: A side note to this lack of cardiovascular training mistake, is spending too much time doing cardiovascular exercise that is endurance oriented. In our sports of USPSA and IDPA, we never run long distances, but often run short sprints from position to position. In light of this, it makes more sense to build a good cardio base, and then focus on speed and agility work during cardiovascular sessions.

> ***Little or no Flexibility*** - Flexibility is a key element needed for just about any skill within a goal oriented shooting training program. This is an area that I see ignored on a regular basis. Any good physical fitness training program

should include elements of flexibility as one of the baseline fitness related training concepts. If you are a practical shooter flexibility will be a huge asset in your program.

> *Lack of Grip and Wrist Strength* - This is a critical part of pretty much all high speed/performance shooting. The top shooters all have grip and tendon strength that is at the upper levels of most athletes. I can remember meeting Jerry Miculek, Rob Leatham, and Phil Strader early in my shooting career and was absolutely amazed by the amount of strength they had when I shook their hands.

Here are the three things that I do to increase my grip, and wrist tendon strength:

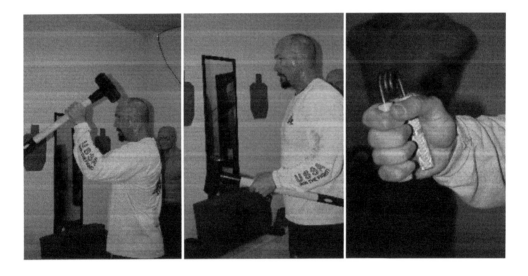

The first exercise strengthens the bottom tendon on my wrist, the second strengthens my forearm and top tendon, and the third (grippers) strengthens my fingers and hands. Other than that, shooting and dry firing both strengthen the hands and forearms when done regularly.

Select Your Program - There are a couple of physical fitness programs that I have personally used over the last several years. These programs are both 12 weeks in length and can easily be modified allowing you to specialize and train the specific components you need within your physical fitness training program for your shooting goal. Either of these programs will build a high level of general fitness, and I strongly recommend doing these programs in the pre or off-season. If you do not have a baseline level of physical fitness, I recommend that you start at the baseline (preparation phases) options within these programs that will train your body and get it ready for the full program. Following these programs exactly as they're written (or videoed) will give you 95% or more of the physical fitness that you will need to meet your shooting goal. The last 5% might be key areas that directly relate to shooting that you feel are not trained thoroughly enough with these programs. An example may be grip strength or wrist tendon strength that is required to build a high performance grip that these programs do not specifically address. It would be relatively easy to address these weak areas with some specific addition of exercises that address those weaknesses.

Timeline - These programs are both twelve weeks in length, and as I already stated should be started in the pre or off-season. The key time to work on your physical fitness is during your off-season. While I may suggest that you emphasize physical fitness during the off-season, in no way am I suggesting that you stop your physical fitness program during the season. You'll simply want to schedule your training sessions so that they don't overlap your matches or competitive events. You should not do a strenuous workout the day of or before a competitive event. Hard physical fitness workouts will create a fatigue known as D.O.M.S. (Delayed Onset Muscular Syndrome) commonly known as extreme soreness. This is a normal byproduct of a strenuous physical fitness workout, especially a strength training session. The last

195

thing we want is to deal with pain and soreness during a competitive event. Your results would certainly suffer.

The Programs - I recommend a couple different physical fitness-training programs, which I have personally used to elevate my fitness levels. I highly recommend that you investigate both programs and utilize them as you see fit. One of the programs is predominantly done as a DVD video-based follow along program, and the other one is in book format. I don't have any association with either of these companies, and they do not sponsor me to say nice things about them. They are simply the best and most diverse workout programs that I have found that will help you elevate your fitness levels without spending hundreds of dollars on personal trainer or exercise equipment.

> ➢ ***Core Performance Workout*** [9] - This program is a very detailed and spans twelve weeks. It incorporates elements of everything needed to perform one's movements well. It is a very detailed program and can be a bit complicated to follow, but it is well worth it. The workout requires relatively little equipment and can be done at home with a few simple pieces of gear. This workout was designed and built upon the premise of developing core strength called "pillar" strength. The author of this program believes and demonstrates that all movements originate around that pillar area consisting of the midsection, lower back, and hips. If you strengthen this area, then the result is better movement mechanics for the entire body. I used this program as a pre-nationals routine several years ago. I did the program later than I should have, and consequently I had to work through the heat of the summer inside my gym (my garage, 95 degrees plus). This may have limited the effectiveness of the program

---

[9] Mark Verstegen, <u>Core Performance</u> (Pheonix: Rodale, Inc, 2004).

a bit, but it sure got me acclimated and used to the heat. Overall, I felt the strongest I have ever felt, and moved better than I have ever moved after completing this program. I do have a series of CD's made by the designer of this program called "Core Essentials", and find those CD's useful, but not necessary if you desire to do the 12-week workout in the book. The only thing I had a hard time with was getting everything done in the amount of time I had, and the number of days per week I had to work out. For you working folks, you understand that getting everything in during the normal workweek can be difficult.

- o Website: http://www.coreperformance.com/
- o Recommendation- Get the book Core Performance and follow the program.

➢ **P90X Workout[10]** - This program is an intense 12-week program that can be followed via DVD. It incorporates a very diverse group of workouts and principles that will increase fitness levels in all key areas. The program requires absolute minimal equipment and will work well to increase strength to weight ratios by reducing body fat. This workout is the primary workout that I use to maintain my fitness levels, along with some supplemental workouts that I have designed myself. The great thing about P90X is that the workout is packaged in a group of twelve DVD's that you just pop in your player and follow along. The main trainer, Tony Horton, is a gifted trainer operating at an incredible fitness level. Trying to keep up with the trainers on the DVD is very inspiring and fun

---

[10] Tony Horton, P90X, 01 01 2004, 01 01 2009 <http://www.beachbody.com/p90x>.

for those wanting a challenge (trust me, I don't care how fit you are, you will be challenged by this one). If you are new to fitness or have some physical limitations, you may want to start with a preparatory program of some sort before starting this program. Make sure you start in the off season for this one, as you will want to have the time to dedicate to building a good base of fitness.

- o Website: http://www.beachbody.com/category/p90x-online.do
- o Recommendation- Get the P90X program and follow the DVD workouts.

Summary: Lets summarize the Physical Fitness section:

- ☐ Physical fitness is a key part of your training program, and there are several components to it. They are:
  - o Strength Training- exercise that increases muscular strength.
  - o Cardiovascular Training- that is exercise that makes the heart and lungs (as well as circulation) work more efficiently.
  - o Plyometric Training- exercise that requires explosive contraction and elongation of the muscle fibers in jumping type moves, that increases the muscles ability to perform those explosive movements better.
  - o Flexibility Training- movements that increase the range of motion of the muscles.
- ☐ Building a physical fitness program can be rewarding, yet complicated and involves several steps such as analyzing your needs, identifying your weaknesses, and selecting program elements that will allow you to perform at your best.
- ☐ There are several common mistakes made by shooters, each of which should be avoided.
- ☐ There are two programs that are complete enough to build serious physical fitness that are recommended with this book:
  - o The P-90X program.
  - o The Core Performance (standard) program.

CHAPTER SEVEN
Visual Training
Module

"If you can't see it, you can't shoot it"

By: Mike Seeklander

The things I will cover in this chapter:

1. *Skills trained in the Visual Training System*
2. *Understanding Visual Skills*
3. *Vision Training Drills*

Visual Training System

<u>Skills Trained</u> - Your visual system (vision) is a key component in your ability to perform well. In this module you will do a set of vision training exercises that will work your eyes just like you would work any muscle in a physical fitness program. First, I will tell you that this part of the program is not mandatory if you are stretched for time. The reason I am not making you do it is that I realize that the other 3-4 parts of this program have already taken a good deal of your time. What I will tell you though, is that vision training might be a key to your success if you have any weaknesses in that area. It has been well demonstrated in professional sports that visual skills sometimes separate the good from the great. I strongly recommend that you take the time to do these visual exercises, and the good news is that you can front load them in the beginning of the season and maintain them with much less effort. As a matter of fact, you can probably put the work in during your pre-season, and during season rely on shooting and dry-firing to keep your eyes in shape.

It is also important that you realize that these exercises are from a compilation of credible sources,[11] [12] and I have validated them and used them myself, but that I am not a doctor. I would encourage you to have you optometrist or eye doctor check

---

[11] Thomas Wilson, <u>SportsVision</u> (Champaign: Human Kinetics, 2004).

[12] O.D. Dr. Wayne F. Martin, <u>An Insight To Sports</u> (Mill Creek: Sports Vision Inc., 1984).

them out first if you have any problems with your vision. On another note, make sure the optometrist you have review them understands the visual demands of our shooting sports. Before I give you the exercises, I need to give you some basic understanding of how your visual system works, and some key terms.

Understanding Visual Skills. The following subcomponents are the skill areas that affect how efficiently our vision works. Realize, that it is very possible to look without "seeing". While most of the areas listed below are completely trainable, you will have to understand there is much more to training your visual systems than just training the small muscles that control the movement of your eyes. You must train them as well as the brain to recognize and react to what the eyes have transmitted to the brain. This connection is absolutely necessary to perform at your best, so do not neglect one component over the other.

> *Static Visual Acuity* - The ability to see to a certain level of detail. This is normally tested by your optometrist by using what is called the Snellen acuity scale. This is the row or rows of letters that the Doctor has you read from a certain distance. If you can successfully read the correct line, a ratio is calculated that results in the term (20/20) or something similar. This simply means that the person can see what a normal person could at 20 feet. Some people have better vision (20/15), and many people have worse (20/100) or more. The larger second number means that the person can see at 20 feet what a normal person could see at 100.

By: Mike Seeklander

➤ *Dynamic Visual Acuity* - This is the ability to see to a certain level of detail while either moving, or looking at a moving object. Obviously, this type of skill is the one we would normally use in most of our sporting applications.

➤ *Visual Motor Skills* - This is the ability to move the eyes efficiently. Without this skill an athlete could not quickly move his eyes to focus on multiple objects. Obviously, this is one of the key areas we can train to increase the speed and consistency with which we move our eyes (and their ability to move together precisely).

➤ *Visual Perceptual Skills* - When we utilize visualization, we are drawing from our visual perceptual skills. Visual perceptual skills are commonly used to remember and have an awareness of diagrams or layouts of a field, court, or a stage at a match. Visual perceptual skills allow you to have an "awareness" of your location as well as the location of other things around you.

➤ *Visual Decisive Skills* - This is the ability to see, recognize, and react to something very quickly. This skill includes much more than visual skills and must be trained by combining vision training along with technical instruction to increase decision-making speed. An example of this is how a top shooter recognizes and makes up a bad shot in much less time than a novice shooter, because of their ability to see, recognize, and decide to shoot another shot is so much faster. The term "visual patience" is directly related to this area, and is a critical element of performing well in our sport. It simply means that the shooter must have the discipline (via training) to wait for the correct visual stimulus (sight picture) before firing. Each sport requires a different set of decision related processes so we must include the elements of our sport in order to train these skills.

➤ *Peripheral Awareness* - Peripheral vision cannot be trained individually, but awareness can be increased through training. Basically our peripheral vision is based on the number of rods and cones in the retina and their ability to detect light. Due to this fact, we cannot improve what is transmitted to the brain, but we can improve our ability to use this information.

➤ *Eye Hand and Foot Coordination* - Coordination between the hand/feet and the eyes is a critical skill for any level of athletic performance. Those people who have better hand/feet eye coordination are normally the ones who naturally excel at the sports they are playing. We naturally train these skills when we do our sport, but they can also be trained in a vision training program.

Types of Vision Training - There are two primary types of vision training both of which will be used in this program.

➤ *Static* - *Static* training is defined as training that takes place in a controlled, non-moving environment. Most sports vision training in a clinical setting will be primarily static in nature. While this training is effective in improving

203

the fundamental aspects of vision, it is not effective if used alone, or at least not as effective as a combination of static and dynamic training methods.

➤ **Dynamic** - Dynamic vision training could be better defined as the vision training while in the environment that the athlete will use their visual skills. Dynamic means moving and this type of training is normally done while moving around and possibly while actually mimicking the activity that we are training for. When performing dynamic vision training, you will effectively "load" the visual systems while creating sympathetic overload. This is important because when we use our trained visual skills, most likely we will have a large variety of sympathetic overloading occurring, and when trained this will make you a much more efficient athlete/operator under the visual stresses you might encounter. Almost all of your dynamic vision training will occur during your live and dry fire training sessions in the drills assigned in those modules if you are using your vision properly and paying attention to the visual cues in each drill.

Balance/Relationship - When we think of training the visual systems, we may not realize the marriage of balance and vision. Most dynamic vision training will incorporate some sort of balancing. Balance can be trained in a variety of ways, but for the purposes of this section, I would like to emphasize sports vision balance, which is the process of working on balancing ability while severely overloading the visual systems. The exercises in your routine can all be done while attempting to improve balance by doing something as simple as standing on one foot.

Vision Training Program - Now that you have a decent understanding of vision and vision exercises, lets get into the program. This program will take you about 15 minutes to do from start to finish.

➤ **Frequency** - Two-three times per day, for three weeks during the pre-season. After this initial strengthening you should be able to maintain by going through the routine two times weekly as a maintenance program during the in-season timeframe. Note: If you feel yourself lacking in your visual skills, increase your training frequency.

- ➤ **Duration** - 15-20 minutes
- ➤ **Routine/exercises** - The following exercises should be done in order. Combined with the load that will be placed on your vision during normal dry and live fire sessions, these primarily static exercises will strengthen any weak areas that you currently have. I recommend that you log your results on certain exercises as well as any other pertinent information you feel important during your vision training sessions.
- ➤ ***Materials Needed – The following list of materials will be needed to perform these exercises:***
  - ○ *Pencil with letters on it.*
  - ○ *Small tennis size rubber ball with 6 circular marks drawn around the equator, and 3 circular marks half way between the equator and poles (north and south poles while holding ball upright). You will have to hang this ball from a string, so a connection point on the North Pole is required.*
  - ○ *Small numbers, ½ inches tall numbering 1-12 (cut into separate pieces)*
  - ○ *One small ½ inch circle with the letter A in the middle of it*

Vision Exercises – As stated above, these exercises should be done in order, and at regular intervals. The initial eye-strengthening program should be done in the pre-season, and then maintained with 2-3 vision training sessions per week. Follow these drills as closely as possible, and consult your Optometrist if you had any problematic side effects such as headaches.

By: Mike Seeklander

Head Roll's	
Purposes	Warm up neck and the small muscles in the eyes.
Materials	None

Procedure: Pick a fixed point 10 feet away, fix your gaze on it and keep your head perfectly still. Perform 10 head rolls clockwise and 10 head rolls counterclockwise while maintaining a clear focus on the fixed point. Don't roll your head so far that you lose the fixed point.

Eye Rotations	
Purposes	Flex and warm up the small muscles in the eyes.
Materials	None

Procedure: Maintain a good posture and look straight ahead. While keeping your head and body still, perform eye rotations by moving your eyes in a circle as wide as your visual field will allow. Rotate 10 times clockwise and 10 times counterclockwise. Try to pay attention to items in your visual field as you do this to increase your awareness in your periphery.

Eye Stretches	
Purposes	Stretch small muscles in the eyes.
Materials	None

Procedure: Maintain a good posture and look straight ahead. While keeping your head and body still, perform 10 repetitions of looking up, right, down, and left as far as you can by just moving your eyes, holding the gaze for one second per spot. One time U, R, D, and L is counted as one repetition.

Push Ups	
Purposes	To stretch the eye muscles that allow the eyes to zoom in and out (cross and uncross)
Materials	Pencil with letters on it.

Procedure: Hold the pencil at arms length with the letters facing you in a vertical position. Find a second point across the room (10 feet or more) and hold the pencil between your eyes and the distant point. Now shift your vision to the fixed object and hold for a count of 3. You should be seeing two blurred pencil images. After the count, shift your vision back to a letter on the pencil, and hold for a count of 3. The distant object should be two blurred images now. That is one repetition. Repeat for 10 repetitions.

Near/Far Eye Jumps	
Purposes	To strengthen the eye muscles that allow the eyes to zoom in and out.
Materials	Pencil with letters on it.

Procedure: Hold the pencil four inches from the eyes centered between them. Pick a second point about 10 or more feet away at eye height. Focus your eyes from a letter on the pencil to the far target back and forth very quickly, ensuring that you see both images with clear focus before you shift. Shift back and forth for 60 seconds and then rest. Repeat 3 times. Try this balancing on one foot for added difficulty.

By: Mike Seeklander

Track the Ball	
Purposes	To build smooth eye movements and tracking ability.
Materials	Small tennis size rubber ball. Attach a string to the north pole of the ball, and draw 6 points around the equator equal distances apart. Halfway between the poles, draw 3 markings equal distance apart around the ball.

Procedure: Hang the ball from a ceiling so it is eye level. Stand far enough away so that it will swing without hitting you. Swing the ball and focus on any point as long as you can with clear vision. When you can no longer see that point, shift focus to one you can see. You may shift focus numerous times. Track the ball with your vision without moving your head. Track a point for 60 seconds. Repeat for another 60 seconds. To make this exercise harder, if you have the ability to attach the ball to a pulley, you can increase and decrease the height of the ball while it swings around.

Multi-Directional Saccades	
Purposes	To increase the ability to jump from one point to another and focus on that point.
Materials	Small numbers made from paper or other material, ½ inch in height, from 1-12, and one small ½ inch circle.

Procedure: Find a large open wall and place the small circle at eye height. Take the remaining 12 numbers and build a clock on the wall with all of the numbers in their correct position approximately 32 inches from the center circle. Begin by standing and looking at the center circle with clear vision. Without moving your head, snap your eyes to the 1 and back to the center circle, then 2 and back to the center, and so on until you have gone all the way around the clock. This in one rotation. Repeat this 5 times. Each time you snap your eyes to a number, stay only long enough to clearly focus on the number before you snap back to center. Time yourself around the clock and try to improve your time, focusing on each number with clarity. Challenge yourself by trying this while standing on one foot.

Other Challenges	
Purposes	Variety.
Materials	None.

Procedure: Try the following eye challenges for fun and additional vision training:

> Try to focus on the reflective markers on the road as you drive by them without moving your head. The closer you get the faster they move! Try the same focusing technique on a crack in the road. Keep your head still while doing these!

> Try to focus on a fan blade and see it clearly while spinning. Ceiling fans work best for this while lying on your back. Some ceiling fans are reversible so you can work both directions.

> Track a fly! Try to focus on and track a fly with your vision without moving your head. This one is tough.

> Track the brass. Try to focus on and follow each piece of brass to the ground as your shooting partner is shooting (or at your next match).

By: Mike Seeklander

Summary: Lets summarize the Visual Training Module:

☐ Shooting well requires good vision, and to increase visual skill, there are several key exercises that can be done.

☐ Visual training can be done for up to three times per day for a period of three weeks, at which time a maintenance program will keep the visual system strong.

☐ Visual base training should be done in the pre-season to get the vision up to the level necessary for the main training phase.

CHAPTER EIGHT
Cross-Training Module

"Cross training may be the key to success"

By: Mike Seeklander

The topics I will cover in this chapter:

1. *Overview of how to switch to another specialty*
2. *Steel Challenge basics (Training tips)*
3. *Bianchi Cup/PPC basics (Training tips)*
4. *Benefits of cross training*

<u>**Using other shooting sports to cross-train**</u> - The "program" was designed to greatly increase your skill level for shooting practical type competitions such as IDPA and USPSA, but the shooting skills that you will gain are certainly usable across the board. One thing about good shooters is that they can use their skill and do pretty good in all of the shooting sports except for the highly specialized sports where there is no skill crossover. Bullseye type shooting would be an example of this, and while there is certainly some crossover of the skills (trigger and sight management to the extreme), the pace is so much slower that we really would not be able to apply practical shooting skills in it, or apply the skills learned in it to practical shooting. There are however, two primary sports that I would consider specialized yet completely applicable and beneficial to practical shooting. If shot, there will be a cross benefit of skills, meaning that the skills you have developed in this program will be useable in them and the skills you will hone while doing them will be useable in your normal competitions. I strongly recommend that you use them as cross training sports, just be careful not to get off track from your primary goals. The two sports I am talking about are Steel Challenge and NRA Bianchi style shooting matches. Training for these matches is quite simple; each of these matches has the same stages each time you shoot. This differs from IDPA and USPSA in that you can memorize the Bianchi and Steel Challenge stages and just focus on those skills that are important on each stage. Conversely, in the IDPA/USPSA sports, we often shoot freestyle stages that require a broad group of generalized skills. My primary recommendation for using them to cross-train (if you decided to shoot

these types of matches) is because of the side benefits you get from training for them.   Individual sport breakdown:

Steel Challenge - The Steel Challenge (SC) is the world speed shooting championship normally held in California. This is an all steel match with 7 stages and 5 targets on each stage, all consisting of round or rectangle steel plates set up at distances from 7-35 yards. The object of SC matches is pure speed and the goal is to hit all 5 targets as fast as possible, with the stop plate last, which records a time for the entire run. The shooter takes either four or five runs, with one throw out run per stage. The times are added together and that is the score for the stage. While pure speed is the goal, accuracy fundamentals are also tested in SC matches because each time you miss a piece of steel, it takes a half second or more to make that shot up. For this reason, it is critical to get a hit with each shot if at all possible. Participating in SC matches will greatly increase your skill in all fundamental shooting skills, but will specifically increase your draw speed and target acquisition speed. For   more   information   on   Steel   Challenge   matches,   visit: http://steelchallenge.com/.

> ***Key Needs: Draw and target transitions*** - Two skill areas will become very important when training and competing in SC matches - draw speed and target transitions. On each stage you will do 4 or 5 separate runs, each requiring a draw (from the surrender position). Each of the stages will also require you to shoot a target once, then move the gun (acquire) to the next one and shoot it. This means that you will do more than 30 draws and over 100 target transitions in the match. The better you are at those two things, the better your overall time is. Let's say for example, that you are doing a draw at about 1.5 seconds average and you decrease your time by a mere two tenths of a second (.2). You would decrease your match score by more

213

than six seconds. This is a huge decrease in time and any professional would give big money for a decrease of that amount. As far as acquisitions, lets say your normal transition time is three tenths of a second (.3), and you decrease that by a mere half of a tenth of a second (.05) to a transition time of a quarter second (.25) per acquisition. You would decrease your match time once again by more than six seconds. Add these two together and we are talking about a decrease in total match time of more than ten seconds (around 11-12). This is a HUGE improvement in a SC score.

Training Tips - Training for the SC is simply a matter of working on the two key skills that I have already listed (draw and transition), and figuring out what order in which to shoot the stages. While training on the stages you will want to break each one down, so you can improve your ability to shoot it on demand well. This requires you to understand and place your focus on certain areas. Here is what I try to do for each stage in the Steel Challenge, and these things should be incorporated in your training:

<u>*Break each stage down for-*</u>

> *Body Position.* Try to find an initial body position that will allow you to get a relatively natural swing through all targets. I like to orient my initial body position on the first or hardest target. I experiment with my foot position to get myself set up to hit the first plate fast and then move through the rest of the plates smoothly. I encourage you to experiment a lot in this area, and take good notes. Log the times and then use the one that works best. When it comes to game day, you will know exactly where to set your feet and consequently body position up for the best results.

➤ *Target Order.* Different shooters like to shoot the targets in different orders. Obviously there are many different ways to shoot them, but on most stages, there are really only a couple good ways. In training you will want to experiment with this and log the results. Try to find a way that is the fastest combined with a higher percentage of hits on the targets. Use the timer to really help you tell the difference. You might find the one that "feels" the best is not the best in the long run.

➤ *Pace.* When training, start at a pace where you can control and get hits on all plates. The importance of hitting the first plate with one shot cannot be underestimated. Once you have found your control zone, start pushing yourself until you can no longer shoot any faster and get hits. Don't spend your time in training shooting at plates and missing, because of course, this will just create bad habits. Learn where you can push on certain stages and where you have to slow down.

➤ *Danger Targets.* All Steel Challenge stages have a couple targets that could be labeled as danger targets. These targets are ones that you are likely to miss, or swing by when you are shooting at them. The biggest danger targets are those that will allow you to swing by them and hit the stop plate before you realized you missed a plate. This penalty is a huge one when shooting the steel challenge, so make sure you learn where these danger targets are based on the order you decide to shoot the stages. Then train yourself to do what you need to do to hit them.

Bianchi Cup/PPC - The Bianchi Cup/PPC matches are matches normally sanctioned by the NRA and referred to as practical pistol matches. They are accuracy intensive

215

By: Mike Seeklander

compared to IDPA and USPSA type matches, and have set courses of fire. Most of the courses can be found on the NRA's website (http://www.nra.org/programs.aspx).

Key Needs: Trigger Control, sight management - Bianchi is an accuracy sport, and this means your sight and trigger management must be awesome to perform well. It also means that your gear must be specifically designed to ensure you have the ability to shoot well at distances up to 50 yards. If your firearm and ammunition is not up to par, then I would strongly suggest experimenting to find a gun and ammunition combination that will allow you to succeed at this match, versus fail just because your gear does not perform well enough.

Training Tips -

➢ *Use the time.* The stages at Bianchi all have PAR times that are relatively slow compared to USPSA/IDPA stage paces. One thing I try to do when practicing Bianchi stages is to use all of the PAR time allotted on that particular string of fire. Since you have been training at the USPSA/IDPA pace, you will likely shoot faster than you need to, and will probably not shoot as accurately as you could if you used more of the PAR time. When training, spend a good deal of time learning how to do this. By the way, you can use a timer when dry firing to improve your ability to learn the pace. Just set up and mimic the stages.

➢ *Work on the key areas that are difficult.* Depending on your skill level, you might find certain things easy on Bianchi stages and some things hard. I would recommend spending your time practicing the hardest stuff and trying to perfect those areas. For example, on the Bianchi plate stage, we shoot all of the way back to 25 yards. The 10 and 15-

yard line may not be difficult for you to clean but the 20 and 25-yard strings are. I would suggest that you spend your time working on the 20 and 25-yard lines rather than wasting that ammunition on the 10 and 15-yard strings. Do shoot through the entire stage (all four strings) a few times for score, after you have worked on and perfected the harder stuff.

> *Track the score, but focus on the skills.* Every time you practice, I recommend you shoot for and track your scores. I think it is important to know what scores you can shoot (so you can track them and watch them improve). I also want to emphasize the importance of focusing on what you have to do to perform well on each stage. This is one of the reasons why you should develop *performance* statements that keep you focused on key components of the stage you are on. I strongly recommend you develop and use them while training for Bianchi events. Using a *performance statement* will help you focus your mind on the skills needed during an event rather than the score you want to shoot.

217

Summary: Lets summarize the Specialty Training Module:

☐ This module was an overview of the specialized sports that directly relate to practical shooting, and how they might be utilized to cross train.
☐ The two main sports covered are:
  o Steel Challenge
  o Bianchi/Action Pistol
☐ Each sport offers and requires specific skills to excel in.
☐ Key needs in Steel Challenge sports-
  o Draw Speed
  o Target Acquisition Speed
☐ Key needs in Bianchi sports-
  o Trigger Control
  o Sight Management
  o Stabilized Shooting Positions

CHAPTER NINE
Documenting Paperwork

"Fail to document, and document your failure"

By: Mike Seeklander

The topics I will cover in this chapter:

1. *Overview of what logs will do for you*
2. *Live Fire logs*
3. *Dry Fire logs*
4. *Match logs*

Purpose: This chapter will discuss the critical nature of documenting your training sessions and game day events. It will introduce you to multiple methods of documentation and discuss each of these, as well as teach you how to integrate the results of those different documenting methods.

Purpose of Documentation - Documentation of training sessions and game day is probably the single most important thing you can do to increase the effectiveness of your training program. I have made the huge error of failing to do this in the past and have regretted not having the ability to look back at my notes and use them to increase the effectiveness of my training program. One thing that really stands out is, I really had no way of knowing if I was improving when I failed to document my training sessions and match results. I thought my training sessions were effective, but did I have the proof? I have since started logging all training sessions and matches just like I am outlining in this section and I have found this to be extremely valuable and usable information when I review it later.

Types of Documentation - When documenting your training sessions and events (game day), you will have a couple options. The first is good 'ole fashioned pen and paper and is the primary method I use to document. The second is video and/or audio documentation of training sessions. I strongly recommend both when you are documenting, because each has its benefits when reviewing data and improving your training processes. If you happen to be a trainer that trains large groups, I recommend that you issue training logs to all of your students and mandate that they use them. Make them document their training so they have a reference later on. In the Marine Corps, we had rifle logbooks issued in boot camp and we used them to log every range session we attended. The Marine Corps was on to something, they knew the importance of being able to reference previous data from training sessions.

Written Logs - Written training and event logs are the simplest and easiest way to document your training sessions. Your written logs should capture everything that is important during your training session. I used to log my data on pre-printed pages that I had in a three ring binder until I developed the logbook "Your Performance Logbook" so that I could capture an entire years worth of training and events in a bound format. (For more information visit my website)

Here are some of the things that you will find in the log pages:

- **Date**: Nothing to explain with this one.
- **Weather Factors**: Capture everything you might want to refer back to, such as temperature, conditions, etc.
- **Gun**: I practice with several different guns, and I always make sure to capture the gun/serial number (I have two of most guns, so if I don't write serial numbers down I will not know which one I shot). This section is important if you have a gun that is failing you in some way (so you know which one to get rid of).
- **Gear**: I train for several different purposes, and depending on what I am training for, I will use different gear. I capture that here.
- **Ammunition**: Always document what ammunition you were using in your session or event. This is important for future reference.

221

By: Mike Seeklander

- **Emotional Control Zone**: This is more of a reminder section for me, but I actually have a block I check off that documents and reminds me of where I need to be in terms of control.

- **Active Visualization**: Another reminder block for me, but I check the box here too (if I did it). I should actively visualize for each drill every session.

- **How I felt**: I like to write down if I am feeling well or not (because it affects my performance).

- **Drill Factors (what, time, hits, notes)**: In this section I capture the actual information I will analyze later. Write each drill down and then document your performance metrics (times, points, etc) as well as any notes you may have on that particular drill. I ALWAYS note if I did something well here, and try to capture why I did it well.

- **Solution Analysis**: I write down overall solutions I found or need to find in future session here. This is a key area I will review before the next session (usually as I am loading my magazines).

- **Success Analysis**: I always take the time to write down something positive here. Even if I am shooting poorly, I find something that went well and emphasize it by writing it down.

Video - Video is the wave of the future. There is nothing comparable to it in terms of having true documentation of what you actually did during a drill or event. In your written documentation you can capture your metrics and how you felt during the performance of your drills, but you don't always get the whole picture. I can't tell you how many times I have seen myself on video and noticed something that I had no idea I was doing. I have also used video to show countless students small things that they are doing wrong, especially when they don't believe they are doing it. I use a tripod and a small, cheap camera to capture my training session drills. If you are really cool, you can spend some money on a camera with a remote, but I have been told that these are hard to find these days (not sure why). This will allow you to set up the camera and then start and stop it with the remote. I set my camera up in a position so I can see as much as possible during the drill. I normally set my gear bag up near the camera so I can get my gun ready and prepare my magazines with ammunition, and then I start the camera and walk out to my shooting spot where I am going to do the drill. You will probably want to mark the spot you are shooting from (or set up a shooting box) so you know you will be centered in the video when you are doing your drill. I don't video my entire sessions, but I do video critical drills that I might be having trouble with.

<u>Analysis of Documentation</u> - Okay, so you are documenting like crazy with written and video logs. You're done with the hard part right. Not so fast. Now we have to use that information that we painstakingly recorded during our training sessions and events. When you review your logs it is important you analyze them correctly, and in a certain order. I will break this down by timeline.

> ➤ ***Post session review*** - This review and analysis is done right after the session, or as soon after as possible. You should review your video first, because what you see may need to be logged into your session or event notes. If you see yourself doing something wrong on the video, enter it in your "solution analysis" written log section. Now review all other notes, and take a moment to transfer key items to the next log you will use, as a reminder for your next training session. Your future session will already be planned, but your notes from this session will affect some of the things you will focus on. If you write down notes on your future log reminding you of some things you want to work or focus on, this will make your next session more effective. Each training log should affect your next session, even if just to validate what you are doing (because it is working).

223

➢ **Pre session review** - This review will be done right before you begin your training session. Look at the last session notes, and also at what you carried over from your last session. You might look at some of your key metrics (times and points) from drills you did so you have some idea of where your metrics should be during this session.

➢ **Monthly review** - I like to take my training session notes out and review them to look for trends on a monthly basis. This will only take a moment, but is really a great way to see if you have some good or bad trends happening. You will also be able to compare your metrics and hopefully see them improving across a month's time. Seeing improvement is a big key to your success! Look for gear and gun issues that seem to be recurring, and any other things that stand out when you look at a month's worth of data. Make sure to take a couple notes on your monthly review and what you found so you can plug that stuff into future sessions. I don't normally recommend changing your program with just one month's data, but do recommend slight changes or increased focus on areas that you notice as problematic.

➢ **Cycle or Yearly review** - I tend to train in 6-12 week cycles. This data review is where you will look for trends that will influence your decision to change your training program. Once again lay all of your data out and take notes on good or bad trends, as well as your performance metrics. You should see some distinct improvement in them after you have been through a complete training cycle, and if not you will want to look hard at your drills and how you are training. No improvement can be a result of many different things, like poor drill design, lack of frequency (you're not training enough), lack of duration (you're not training long enough), etc. The notes from this review will be what you use to modify your program.

Program Measurement - How do we measure whether or not our training program is working? Actually it's quite simple; we simply look at the results on game day to assess our performance. As stated in a previous chapter, game day is the event for which you are training. If you are improving, your results will show it, if not, you will see that too.

Failures Reflected Upon - Don't get caught in the trap of measuring your success or failures based on how you felt you did during an event. ALL issues that happen to you during your performances are a result of how you train. If you tank, and mentally crash in certain areas, then you trained yourself to do exactly that. If your physical skills are not where they should be, and you have mistakes or failures because of them, then your training program caused that. Don't get in the habit of just thinking you had a bad day because your preparation should be thorough enough to get you through any "bad day" without any huge problems. We *prepare* ourselves to perform on a "bad day" by minimizing or eliminating them. You might be thinking that I am saying that if you have developed your training program correctly and executed it perfectly, you will be mistake free. Not so, I am simply saying that you will make errors on the scale that you allowed them to happen based on how you trained. You can make errors and still succeed in your shooting goal, but they have to be minimal, and you have to be able to react and flow through them. Big errors should not happen much, if at all, if you trained right. Now, I am not saying that you will reach this well trained state overnight. It may take ten years of hard training to get to the level where you are performing to your ability relatively mistake free.

As much as I have not wanted to take responsibility in the past for my own mistakes on game day, when I reflected back and analyzed my training program, I always found the flaw. No problem, because the training design cycle is a *cycle*. The

By: Mike Seeklander

concept is that you are in a never-ending loop of perfecting your performance by perfecting your training program and its efficiency.

Program Modification - All training programs should be evaluated and modified at some point, and I recommend that this occurs at least every sixteen weeks or so. In this particular program, some of you might be advanced enough to modify certain things right away, but I strongly caution you against this until you have gone through it in its entirety.

Here is a visual of the program learning and modification cycle:

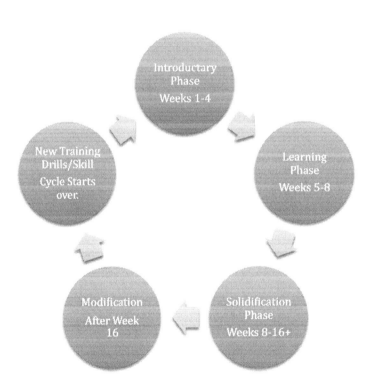

Objective Assessment - I am a firm believer that doing an objective assessment of your performance is the only way to go. We've established that measuring your performance will happen in one of two ways, either you will look at your game day performances (i.e. the quizzes (local matches) you take along the way to the big test (major match), or go through some sort of skills test that you have established as a measurement tool for the skills you will need to have to accomplish your major goal. Once we've gone through either of these two tests, it's incredibly important that you look at the results objectively and have the ability to take those results and modify your training program. By objectively I mean that you look at results and compare them to some sort of documented metrics or rely on video review to ensure that you are looking at what is actually happening, rather than how you "feel" you are doing. In order to have these metrics, you will have to be disciplined in how you set up your training drills as well as the documentation of the results.

Modification of the Program - Okay, you have completed the majority or all of a 16-week cycle and you have documented your training sessions. You have taken some game day quizzes along the way and documented them, too. Now what? Let's look at that critical data and begin the process of modification. One great thing about this step is that it will both increase your program's efficiency as well as give you a fresh and new set of objectives and training drills. Even if you have just modified your initial drills they will still be different and possibly more challenging (hopefully), which will stimulate a new learning curve. There are some logical steps in analyzing your results and modifying your program.

It doesn't matter if you met your goal or did not succeed, you will still want to go through these steps and modify your program where it needs to be modified. This will allow you to continually push to meet your goal or reach for the next level. There is always a next level.

> *Step one*. Review your training logs. Don't have any? You're stuck. Seriously, that is why you must log your training sessions. If not, you are on a dead end training road. O.K., so what are you looking for? Trends?

227

Solutions to statements? What you did really well? Lack of improvements in your numbers from one session to the next? If you took good notes, it will all be right there for you to act on and use to modify your training program for the better. Write all of these trends and statements down on one sheet, if possible, so you can view it all at a glance.

> *Step two*. Take your notes and separate them into different areas. Each area will affect what you modify in your program. For example, if you find that you consistently documented that you did a certain skill really well, you might want to work less on that skill in future training sessions. You might take the drill that trains that skill and remove it or lessen the frequency that you do it. I would rather spend the time working on something I noted as something I needed to find a solution for, than waste my time working on something I am already good at. By the way, this is not human nature. We would much rather work on things we like than things that are not fun to us. Make sure to categorize drills for which you lack improvement. This indicates that something is not working with the drill, or maybe it is possible that you are "maxed" out on that skill and have no room to grow (this is very rare). Either way, you may need to look at those specific drills and modify them.

> *Step three*. Modify your program based on what you noted above. The key areas that will likely need to be modified are: training drill specifics (not meeting their goal of improving your metrics) and training session layouts (frequency, duration, drills used). Modification will require some common sense and time, since you are reworking your training program. Modify drills to better suit your needs, and modify your training session

layouts so that it does what you need it to as reflected in your notes. This may be more of one drill and less of another, and possibly even the design and addition of a completely new drill. If you have done your job in documenting, you will simply follow your notes.

> ***Step four***. You must validate. Before you go to the trouble of printing out your new training plan in its final version, with your modified drills and sessions, go to the range and use them once. You will catch things that are not working out as well as you might have thought. Note your changes, make them, and then finalize the drills and begin another training cycle.

Modification of your training program should be ongoing and never ending. As you continually evolve and improve, so will your training program. Modify your drills so that they continue to challenge you and keep you on your performance edge. The better your training program is, the more you will increase your skill because you will become more efficient at training. This will lead to superior skills in the long run.

Training Log Pages - Please see the next pages for some shortened sample live fire, dry fire, and event (match) logs. Also, if you would like to use these logbook pages, please visit my website for information on ordering "Your Performance Logbook".

By: Mike Seeklander

Training Log - General Details

DID YOU REVIEW YOUR LAST TRAINING LOG FOR KEY INFORMATION BEFORE BEGINNING??

Session: _____ Date: _____ Weather: Sunny Cloudy Rain Snow Windy Temp:_____

Gun: _____ Problems: Y N Ammo: _____ Holster/Rig: IPSC - IDPA – Carry

Video Taken: Y N   Emotional Control Zone (overall): 1 - 2 - 3   Did Active Visualization? Yes - No

Today I felt: Great Good Mediocre Sick

Drill:										Totals
Times										
Points										
Key Notes										

Drill:										Totals
Times										
Points										
Key Notes										

Success Analysis: (What I did really well)

_____

_____

Solution Analysis: (What I figured out or need to figure out)

_____

_____

General Notes: (Any additional notes on the training session)

_____

_____

Match Event Log -General Details

Event: _____ Date: _____ Weather: Sunny Cloudy Rain Snow Windy Temp: _____

Gun: _____ Problems: Y N Ammo: _____ Holster/Rig: IPSC - IDPA – Carry

Video Taken: Y   N   Emotional Control Zone (overall): 1 - 2 - 3   Did Active Visualization? Yes - No

Today I felt: Great   Good   Mediocre   Sick   Overall Finish: _____   Accuracy %: _____   Penalties: _____

GM/Professionals at match (to help track my finish against them):
_____

Performance Metrics

Training Program addition/modification: (drills I need to add or modify based on analysis above)_____
_____

Success Analysis: (What I did really well, I can minimize training in these areas)_____
_____

Gear: (How my gear did)_____
_____

Stage Overview:

Stage	Time	Points	Penalties	Hit factor	%/Finish

Stage:					Finish:
Time		Points		Penalties		Control Zone	
Key Notes					

Copyright 2010 Shooting-Performance   By: Mike Seeklander

Dry Fire Log

Session (A, B, C, D, Other): _____Date: _____

MTTS: Maximum Technical Training Speed (100% of your potential speed, while doing the technique completely correct).

Before you begin:

  ➢ Focus Breath (key touch point and 6-2-6)
  ➢ Run your visualization video (passive, personal success video)
  ➢ Use Active visualization in between your drills, see yourself do it and then do it.
  ➢ Use your *performance statement* and read your *self image booster* (should be on a 3x5 index card in your shooting bag)

Preparing for:		
Gun/Gear (IDPA, USPSA, Etc.):		
Dry Fire Drill	*Beginning MTTS PAR Time*	*Ending MTTS PAR Time*

Today's goal statement: (Where I want to go)_____
_____
_____

Notes: (Anything else)_____
_____

Summary: Lets summarize the Documenting Paperwork section:

- ☐ Documenting will be one of the keys to your success.
- ☐ Documenting sheets can be found in "Your Performance Logbook", in a preprinted published format that will allow you to log any session or match.
- ☐ The three types of log pages are:
    - ○ Dry Fire Logs- Designed to help you log your dry fire sessions.
    - ○ Live Fire Logs- Designed to help you log your live fire training sessions.
    - ○ Match/Event Logs- Designed to help you log your matches/events for future analysis of the information.

233

CHAPTER TEN
Game Day Performance

"If your training was correct and thorough, it will be reflected on game day"

By: Mike Seeklander

The topics I will cover in this chapter:

1. *General Thoughts*
2. *Pre-Game preparation*
3. *During-Game Actions*
4. *Post-Game must do activities*

Game Day Performance

<u>**General**</u> - Even though your game day (match) performance is really based on how you train, there are better ways to approach a match rather than just go shoot it. For this reason I thought I would write a short section of all of the things that are important on game day. I want you to maximize your performance so you can validate or modify your program as necessary. Think about using any match you shoot as a quiz that will help you really measure where your skills are, and how your training program is doing. Without these quizzes on a regular basis, you won't be able to assess whether your program is working or not. Believe it or not, even when I shoot a large state level match, I think of it as a quiz for the next bigger match. This mentality allows me to reduce the pressure at that particular match to an extent, and is a technique I recommend you try. For example, if I shoot a club match, I look at it as preparation for the state match. When I shoot the state championship, I look at it as preparation for the area championship. When I shoot the area championship, I look at it as preparation for the national championship. When I shoot the national championship, I look at it as preparation for the world championship. I could go on and on, but the point is that I take the stress inducing importance of the match out of my mind, which allows me to relax and shoot better. It also equalizes all matches and I tend to treat a club match like a championship match. Most of you do better at club matches anyway, right? Why not trick your brain to think all matches are the same so that you don't put large amounts of pressure on yourself at one particular match?

Pre-Game - What you do before the match, within about a seventy-two hour window will certainly have an effect on your performance. I will break this down into a few sections.

> *Nutrition and Hydration* - First of all, you will want to take the time to fuel your body right so your energy levels are up. Don't make the mistake of thinking you can eat a great meal the morning of the match and be ok, because it's too late! Your body has already processed the food in your stomach from days before and plans on using that as fuel, not what you ate for breakfast. However, that breakfast is still important though as it too will contribute to your overall energy levels and how you feel. Drinks lots of water to hydrate before the match, up to seventy-two hours before the match, especially if it is going to be hot. Please don't underestimate the effects that dehydration will have on your performance. Stay away from alcoholic beverages the night before, and maybe even a couple days before.

> *Practice and Preparation* - Your practice sessions for the match should not change much. If you are shooting a local event, I want you to treat that like another training session for that week. However, for a major match, I want you to hit all of your scheduled sessions up to seventy-two hours before the match and then stop. You may shoot a bit after that, but I don't want you to be tired or burned out the day of the match. My routine is to practice up to seventy-two hours before the match and then if I shoot after that, it is only to zero my gun, check ammunition, etc. I do however recommend that you continue to dry fire up to the match, just don't overdo it. The great thing about dry firing versus live firing before a match is that when you dry fire you can't miss. Live fire practice right before a match might have negative effects if you shoot bad that day. The exception might be something like

237

Bianchi or the Steel Challenge where we normally hit the practice range right up to the hour of the match.

➢ **The Training/Match Relationship** – This is a key component in performing your best at matches, and is a simple one to use. Simply take the time to look over your training notes and make sure that you are applying the skills you have in practice to the match, as well as your limitations. The best time to use this is during your stage planning process. For example, if you are a really good shooter while moving, then you can plan more movement on stages than someone who is weak in that area. Maybe you are not challenged at all by longer shots and do quite well on them during training, and you have the opportunity to use some longer shots to save yourself significant time on a stage, then do so. Conversely, if you know you have problems with a key technique in training, and that you have not perfected it, then use that knowledge in your planning if you find that technique required at a match. Pay particular attention to that area on the stage, so you can be sure you succeed.

➢ **Gear and Equipment Check** - As far as preparation goes, do use the seventy-two hour window before a match to check, and double check gear, guns, and ammunition. Your complete break down of the gun should occur here, and you should also be drop checking (making sure each round will fit in a chamber gauge made for your caliber) your ammunition. Make sure you have a packing list prepared if you are traveling. Check and clean your magazines and all other gear

➢ **Stage/Match Recon** - If at all possible, you need to get to the match early enough to recon the layout of the match stages, as well as the stages themselves. You might think you can use published stage diagrams to plan for the stages, but this is wrong. Most are not even close to correct. The only stage diagrams that I have ever seen that could be used to plan with were ones done by Tim Egan who ran the Area 1 match for a couple years, his stage diagrams where unbelievable, and completely correct. (With multiple views!) This is a critical component that I have skipped in the past and paid the price. This is a very important part of your mental preparation and planning that will help you shoot much better. If possible (check with the match director), I recommend that you get to the match early and check in. Normally they give you a match booklet of all stages during check-in, which is a very valuable tool when you are scouting the stages. If not, bring a notebook and sketch the stages and key information. Try to get a loose plan together on how you will shoot most of the stages, and if you have a schedule, try to note what the light conditions are going to be like when you shoot. If you are shooting a USPSA match, there will normally be props involved so try to get a look at how they work and where they move. I don't recommend you finalize your plan on your recon session, since you might change it when you are actually with your squad and you don't want to have a plan programmed into your head that you may change. Just get a feel for where each shooting position and target is, and what they look to be in terms of distance. This will allow you to start to build a conscious memory of the stage so final planning will be much faster when you are there to shoot.

During Game – The top shooters tend to "work" a match. You might have noticed that I said "work" a match rather than "shoot" a match. This is because if you are doing what you should be doing, you are really going to be working to keep yourself prepared for the next stage and then perform on it when the time comes. Here are the important points to working a match:

> *Stay consistent* - The more things you do the same, the better your chances of performing well, and staying in a positive, comfortable state. This includes

239

trying to stay consistent with your practice sessions (they should mimic how you operate at a match right?). Load the same; prepare your magazines the same, etc.

> **Shooting order** - Know when it will be your turn to shoot. This will allow you to go through a focus breath and success statement as well as multiple active visualizations before you shoot.

> **Visualize** - Do not skip this. I can't believe how many shooters I meet that do not know how to visualize. This is really important. We discussed active visualization in the mental section. Use the technique. You should be able to face away and see yourself shoot the entire stage (at speed correctly) without opening your eyes.

> **Prepare** - Once you are done shooting a stage, it is not time to relax. It is time to prepare. The next stage will be on top of you before you know it. Prepare (clean and load) your magazines. Glance at your gun to ensure it is good (I have done a quick glance and noticed a rear sight pin drifting out). Re-apply grip goo (pro-grip or whatever). Look at your match booklet for notes you took on the upcoming stage about danger areas, etc. If there are props on the stage and you are close enough to see the stage, try to sneak a look at them and how they operate.

> **Scout and final plan** - When you get onto the next stage, wait for the briefing before you make your final plan. You might get guidance from the RO on something you did not know previously. Then go ahead and scout each position to check and see if anything has changed from your previous recon. Once done, finalize your plan and begin to visualize it, over and over. Don't stop visualizing until you are convinced you are ready. IF you have done all of the above, and are really ready to shoot the stage, take a minute and relax!

> **Stay fed and hydrated** - I will keep this simple and short. I buy nutrition bar's that have a carbohydrate/protein mix in them so I don't get an energy

spike and drop, and I take two bites at a time 2-3 times per hour. Small bites like this keeps my blood sugar stable and my energy high. I also constantly sip water and stay away from Gatorade and sugar drinks. You need to do both of these consistently during the match; they are big keys to performing well. I have and have seen other good shooters fall off the edge because they don't follow this simple plan.

Post-Game - Ok, now its time to capture all of that key data and squeeze that brain for information that you might not remember later. Get your match log out and document the details of how it went. You should also review your video and document anything that you noticed. This might include things you performed well or need improvement on. Remember that you will use your logbook notes to modify and possibly change your future training sessions, so you will want to make sure your match logs are done right, and are thorough.

By: Mike Seeklander

Summary: Lets summarize the Game Day Performance section:

☐ Game day (match performance) will depend on your training, as well as your pre-game preparation. This can be broken down into three distinct areas:

- o Pre-Game preparation- this is the preparation you will go through to get ready for the event, the 24 hours before it happens. This includes diet and hydration.
- o During Game actions- These actions are key things you will want to do in order to make you more successful during the event, as well as after it. Make sure you:
  - ▪ Stay consistent
  - ▪ Know your shooting order
  - ▪ Use proper visualization
  - ▪ Prepare your gear between stages
  - ▪ Scout the stage
  - ▪ Continue your hydration and food intake
- o Post Game actions- These actions are the things you need to do as soon as you are done shooting, to increase your effectiveness at improving your training program.

☐ Treat game days (matches) as preparation for the next one, and try not to overemphasize the event and make it more than it is in your mind.

Bonus 1
Selecting and
Setting Up Your
Guns and Gear

"Its not about the gun"

By: Mike Seeklander

The things I will cover in this chapter:

1. *Firearm Selection*
2. *Gear Selection*
3. *Firearm and Gear Modification*

<u>Purpose:</u> This chapter will show you how to pick the proper equipment including the key ingredient, firearms. Initially, I wanted to avoid trying discussing gear selection in this book because it is so subjective, but decided to add this section to pass on the material that I have learned over the years. I will try to show you how to avoid the equipment race, and try to give you some tips on gear. Please understand that this gun and gear section will benefit those who compete in practical types of shooting events the most.

Firearm Selection. This is always one of the first questions people will ask when they are gearing up, and often shooters want to know what gun I like the most. The answer usually surprises them when I tell them that it really does not matter as long as they observe a few key rules. Now, don't get me wrong, there are some firearms that I like a lot more than others, but in general, the reason I like them better is that they exceed in one or all of the areas listed below. One thought you may have a hard time swallowing is the fact that "it's not about the gun" when you look at who is performing well and who isn't. One top shooter who has proven the belief that a great athlete can win with any gun is Dave Sevigny. Dave has been at the top of the finishes at every major match he has shot in the last 5 years or more, and has won multiple national championships while competing with a nearly stock Glock handgun against the full race guns built for use in the USPSA Limited class. While today there are multiple production type guns that compete evenly with Glocks, Dave proved the fact that a production type gun could beat the race guns out there with a good shooter behind them. While I credit Dave as a super athlete, there are

244

others that have competed and finished quite well with what seem like inferior handguns competing against full custom guns. The point is, that in order to perform well, you must remember that the gun is simply a tool, and the best athletes excel because of their skill, not because they use a specific gun. They may have their preferences, but they can apply the skills they have spent years developing with just about any gun.

Key Considerations. When selecting a firearm, there are some key considerations (listed below), but one thing you need to figure out first is what purpose the gun will serve. If you are reading this book, it is highly likely that you plan to compete with the gun, and you may be planning to "dual use" the gun, which is when we have a carry gun that will be used in practical type shooting matches. I describe three factors below that are in my order of priority, but depending on your planned use for your gun, the priority of these items may be different. For example, if you are shooting a bull's-eye type sport where accuracy is an absolute must, and malfunctions are given an alibi (reshoot to make up for the malfunction), you may prioritize your gun selection based on accuracy. For me, reliability is number one, because in practical type matches, as well as my secondary use for most of my guns (self defense), reliability is very, very important. Take some time and prioritize what you need first, then select a gun based on that and remember that the training done with the tool, i.e. the mental factors behind the skill are what really allow people to perform at the highest level, not the gun itself.

I STRONGLY recommend picking one model of handgun or rifle that will meet all of your priorities and needs, and spend your time and money (for ammunition) on that one gun. If you carry a particular type of gun for self-defense, or while on duty if you are in the military or law enforcement, then I highly recommend competing with that gun, or at least the same model. If you are a very experienced shooter, then you

By: Mike Seeklander

can make the decision to switch back and forth between different guns, but the new shooter should stick to one thing. This will allow you to focus on developing fundamental skills to an advanced level rather than chasing equipment and the newest gun or holster. I have seen huge amounts of time and money wasted on the proverbial gun and gear chase; don't be that guy/gal. Here is what you need to look at when selecting a firearm for competitive or combative purposes, listed in order of priority:

> *Reliability*. The number one thing a firearm must do is work. Nothing else matters if you have malfunctions during matches or during a fight. Most good production guns *should* be very reliable out of the box, and with a good gunsmith custom guns should work every time. If they don't work, get rid of them. You will want to pay particular attention to the ammunition you use, and the magazines you use to feed that ammunition into the gun, because the large majority of malfunctions are indeed caused by faulty ammunition or magazines, NOT the gun. If you know without a doubt that the magazines and ammunition are good, and the gun fails, then it is time to do some trading. Actually, if the gun is a carry gun, do someone a favor and get the gun fixed if possible before trading it, or at least let them know what they are getting so they don't stake their life or competitive resume on the gun.

> *Ergonomics*. The second thing I look for in a firearm is its physical design and ability to be shot well. Generally a gun with a low bore to axis ratio will recover better during recoil because this low axis causes the recoil to travel straight back and through the arm, rather than up. The recoil has to go somewhere, and a well designed gun will recoil considerably less. The slide lock lever, magazine release, and other manipulation devices should be located in easy to reach and

operate spots. If you purchase any high quality production firearm made by a reputable company, these items won't be a problem. Ambidextrous operating devices are preferred, and at a minimum the safety, if the gun has one, should be located and operable on both sides of the gun. If you have a choice, you should select a single action (or similar) trigger design for the first and following shots, as double action first shots are tough when we have to hit a small target. Interchangeable grips are a new concept and allow shooters with bigger or smaller hands to customize their guns. The best test of ergonomics is to shoot the gun and try to manipulate it while shooting. You will find noticeable differences in different designs.

➤ *Accuracy.* Accuracy is third on my list because while it is important, in the practical shooting sports it is not the most important factor. Even so, I am pretty particular about at least having a gun that will shoot as good or better than I am able to shoot it. Guns should be capable of shooting a group of three to four inches at 25 yards at a minimum, and if they can't, athletes should research aftermarket barrels to try to increase accuracy.

What caliber should I choose? If you are going to use your gun for dual purposes, then this may be pretty important to you. You will want to select a caliber that works for self-defense and is also good for whatever type of competitive match you plan to shoot. In general, in the different sports there will be certain limiting factors posted in the rulebooks that will guide you to choose and shoot a particular caliber. Check out the rulebook for your sport and find out if there are minimum calibers or power factors. Power factor is a concept that came from early IPSC matches where the sport creators wanted to ensure that athletes where using ammunition that

247

By: Mike Seeklander

closely simulated carry type ammunition. If there are no caliber requirements or power factor requirements, then I recommend selecting a caliber that is cheap and easy to find, such as 9mm NATO. This will allow you to purchase ammunition if you have not made the decision to reload yet, and will save you lots of money and time.

Firearm Setup. The set up of the gun is critical to how it performs. First, you must know what is legal within your sport prior to modifying a gun in any way. Different divisions and sports will require dramatically different firearm setups. Here are the key factors that should be dealt with when setting up a gun:

> *Trigger* - Most trigger weights are very heavy on stock guns, and should be lightened considerably (for competition guns only, not carry guns). Trigger weights of 2-3 pounds are very manageable and will increase an athlete's ability to manipulate the trigger without disturbing the sights. Trigger type and length should also be considered. If possible, you should have a trigger length that allows you to place your trigger finger on the trigger with no more than a 90-degree bend in the second joint. Note: Be very careful if you plan to use your competition gun for carry purposes, especially if you have a light trigger on it (something I don't recommend).

> *Sights* - Sight modification is critical if you expect to do well. Most factory sights are junk and should be replaced. Visibility is a big factor for competition sights. There are several manufacturers who make fiber optic sights that will allow an athlete to see their sights better in all light conditions. Modifications of the front and rear sights include replacing the front with fiber optic sights as well as narrowing them. Rear sights should be opened up and cut deeper to allow the athlete to see more of what the front sight is doing during recoil. You want to create a big window to look through when modifying or replacing your sights.

> *Grip Surfaces* - All allowable grip surfaces should be stippled or coated with skateboard tape except for the back strap of the gun. The backstrap of the gun should be left relatively smooth to allow the strong hand to index the gun properly and slide up to a high grip position on the tang of the weapon. Athletes should check the IDPA or USPSA rulebooks to ensure they are meeting the obligated rules of respective divisions. The area under the trigger guard, approximately one inch from the bottom of the trigger guard should be left free of stippling or tape, to allow the middle finger to slip into the proper grip when performing a table type draw.

> *Manipulation devices* - (Check rulebooks first!)
>   o *Magazine release-* An extended magazine release should be considered for those who cannot reach the button without pivoting the gun in their hand. Athletes should be sure to test the gun after fitting an extended release to ensure the release is not depressed when pressing down on the gun during a table top draw. An extended release may also be hit with the support hand during the gripping process and may cause the magazine to fall out of the gun.
>   o *Slide Lock/Release lever-* An extended slide lock/release lever should be considered for those who cannot reach the release without moving the gun in their hand. Athletes should consider using the support hand thumb to activate the release in some cases, although when shooting with the strong hand only this will not work. Another thing that you might consider is modifying guns so the slide lock lever is deactivated. Most limited division

249

guns have this modification done because it prevents the malfunctions that occur from having an active slide lock (the SV/STI type pistols are prone to this). This modification is not necessary if you don't have that problem.

Firearm Maintenance

General Cleaning - I recommend that athletes clean their guns as much as necessary to keep them running and to reduce wear. I do not recommend that anyone waste their time cleaning guns every time they are used unless the wear factor is high because of some element from the environment. While I do not want to recommend that shooters go against any type of warranty that their firearm manufacturer recommends, I would have a hard time believing that there is any significant additional wear on a firearm that is not cleaned every time it is shot. A couple important details though:

- *Keep the gun oiled well, on all wear points.* This will go along way in keeping a gun in good running condition. I have guns that have gone well over 50,000 rounds and show no noticeable wear because I oil my guns during practice sessions. This keeps the key areas lubed and friction low, which decreases wear.

- *Wipe any abrasive material from wear points.* This is not what I call cleaning a gun, just a quick wipe down removing dust or grime, sometimes while the gun is still fully intact. Even if you disassemble the frame/slide, you will spend a total of 3-4 minutes doing this and will reduce wear by a large percentage.

Detailed Cleaning - A detailed cleaning should be done prior to any large important event, or even before local matches if the gun is extremely dirty. It is important that you do everything you can to avoid gun problems during a match that may be caused by a dirty gun. There is absolutely no excuse for losing a match due to gun problems caused by failure to clean a gun. If you plan to use the gun for self-defense or purposes other than competing, then making sure it is serviceable is very important.

Detailed Inspection/Parts Replacement. A detailed inspection and possible parts replacement should be done yearly during the off-season. For a gun that is shot more than 25,000 rounds, an inspection should be done sooner. I realize that this is a lot of wear and tear, and well over some manufacturers recommended inspection point, but good guns that are taken care of should be fine. A good gunsmith, or certified gun technician should be enlisted to help with this process, as they will catch problems that the untrained eye won't.

Belt, Holster, Magazine Pouch Selection and Set up.

Holster Selection. Selection of a good holster is critical when choosing your gear. This subject seems simple enough, and if you are reading this and have already spent some time in your sport, then you can probably skip ahead of this section. The one thing that always amazes me is the number of athletes that I see at matches, (as well as professionals who carry a gun for a living) that use some junk type of holster that probably costs about $15. I admit that I used a duty holster with the snaps cut

251

off for some time when I got into the sport, but that did not last any longer than my first match when I realized how much better equipment there was out there. I know you may not have a bunch of extra money to spend, but it is well worth spending to get good gear when you start out. I know money is tight these days, but the holster I use costs about $39.00 and can be used for IDPA and USPSA (the Safariland 5188 is my primary holster for almost everything I shoot now). There is some absolute junk out there, and some stuff that if used for carry purposes, may get you hurt or killed. Hear me now, if you care at all about your performance, then spend some time researching and buy a good set of gear to begin with. Don't waste your time clowning around with junk that will frustrate you and not get the job done. If you plan on dual use of your firearm and gear, then selection is pretty simple. Carry and compete with the same gear. If you rely on your skills to save your life, I would seriously consider using the same gear across the board. This will ensure you are training with your duty (carry) gear, and since you are not going back and forth you will be that much better with it. Although having the right gear for competitive use is a plus, it does not separate the winners from the losers, skill does. Just like with your selection of a firearm, "it's not about the gear." Use your duty (carry) gear for dual use for at least your first year or two competing. Here are some selection criteria to pay attention to:

> *Legal within your sport and division.* (Check rules books, or simply ask some experienced competitor if you can't find one).
> *Designed for the purpose you intend to use it.* This may mean a specific race holster in a sport where hundredths of seconds count when drawing the gun.
> *Heavy-duty construction.* NONE of the reputable manufacturers out there make junk. Flimsy, plastic, cheap mounting hardware, etc. are all signs of cheap products and are guaranteed to break or malfunction.

> *Securely Mounted.* Depending, once again, on what division or sport you shoot, this might be different for each individual. The bottom line is that however the holster mounts to the belt, it MUST be secure. A gun that moves around because the holster does not mount well will be harder to draw. I use extra screws to mount some of my holsters securely, and ensure they stay in the same position.

> *Low Friction.* Speed is pretty important in most firearm sports! This is going to be more important if you perform a bunch of draws in your sport, and if your sport does not require drawing the handgun, then this is not important. Most of the sports that I know of require that the handgun be drawn from a holster, and in this case low friction is a key. You do not want to have to fight the holster for the gun! Holsters of a Laminate or Kydex of type design fit this requirement and there are multiple materials that manufacturers use today to make holsters. While the leather holster of yesterday is not gone, it is certainly not used as much in competition!

> *Lockable.* This means that I want to have a design feature that allows me to lock the gun in the holster, if possible. If the holster does not have this, then I prefer one with some sort of friction tension screw where I can increase the friction in cases where I may have to move or run with the gun in the holster. I can't stand the feeling of a holster that might lose my gun if I bump it. I have had guns fall out of holsters before and prefer it doesn't happen again.

253

➢ *Adjustable.* If the division that you are shooting allows it, you will want to adjust the holster so that is allows fast access and a streamlined draw. If possible, I want a holster that I can adjust for height and cant angle, at a minimum. The full race holsters made today are adjustable for almost any angle.

Magazine Pouch Selection - Carrying your spare ammunition is something that you may be able to do without magazine pouches, but anyone who competes in practical type matches and those who carry for combative purposes will have to select magazine pouches that will meet their need. For combative (carry) purposes, magazine pouch selection is pretty simple so I will only break down selecting them for competitive purposes.

➢ *Legal in the sport/division.* You will find that some sports/divisions require the magazine be covered up to a certain point, or completely enclosed by the pouch/carrier. To find out what is required in your sport/division, consult the rulebooks. If you plan on competing in multiple sports, try to find a pouch/carrier that you can dual use. I compete in many different sports and divisions within those sports, and the one thing that I hate the most is switching gear back and forth. As of the last year or so, I stick to one or two basic setups, even if I have to steer always from my old full race rig. I have not found this to hamper my performance in any way, and have observed several other top shooters doing this, too.

➢ *Adjustable for cant.* This is once again dependent on the rules. If they allow it, having adjustability in a magazine pouch is a great thing. Every one of us is built different and it is nice to be able to adjust the magazine pouch so that your palm indexes it correctly each and every time.

> *Adjustable for tension.* Most good manufacturers make magazine pouches with some sort of tension screw which allows you to increase or decrease tension. I have seen many athletes run down a stage leaving a trail of magazines along the way. I will actually increase or decrease tension on the magazine pouch depending on what type of stage or match I am on. Obviously, "loose is fast" (a key phrase Phil Strader uses), but sometimes "loose is lost" if you have to get aggressive in your movement. By the way, if you are dual using the gear, for combative purposes you will want magazine pouches that really retain the magazines.

Belt System Selection - The most commonly overlooked piece of gear is the belt/system on which you mount your gear/holster. The belt is the foundation of the holster and magazine pouches. If the belt does not securely hold those items, then they will move around and bind, which will mean that your draw is not going to be good, and when you access your magazines, that won't go well either. I have seen more $10.99 Wal-Mart leather belts holding hundreds of dollars worth of holster and magazine pouches than I care to remember, and normally the person has a $2000 custom gun secured by that same belt. Buy a good belt, one made to carry firearm related gear. Here are some things you may find/consider when selecting a belt system. (I say system, because most of us are using an inner/outer belt system for divisions where they are legal versus a standard belt.)

> *Inner/Outer Velcro belt system.* Most of the manufacturers are making belt systems that are composed of an inner belt that goes through your belt loops, and an outer belt that covers the inner

255

belt and is secured together by Velcro. The outer belt simply wraps around the inner belt and "sticks" to it. These systems make for easy on and easy off and are used almost predominantly by shooters competing in the shooting sports where it is legal. Another great advantage to these systems is the ability to switch to a completely different set of gear/gun combination by simply ripping the outer belt off and wrapping a new one on. The holster and magazine pouches are already pre-mounted and stay on the outer belt. I strongly recommend one of these types of systems if it is legal in your division/sport (yeah, rulebook again). Obviously, these systems are not meant for combative use.

➢ *Standard belt.* There is absolutely nothing wrong with using a standard leather belt to mount your gear on. Some sports/divisions require that you use a standard belt. The key is finding one that is reinforced and designed to carry gun gear. Safariland makes a good leather belt, for example, that has reinforcement panels in both the holster area and magazine pouch area of the belt. There are several manufacturers out there that are making a canvas type belt with a loop buckle that have reinforced areas in the sides for the holster and magazine pouch. These too make great belts, and the advantage with them is that they can be cinched down in micro adjustments versus having to cut more holes in a leather belt with a normal buckle.

Holster and Magazine Pouch Adjustment - Once you have selected your gear, you will need to set it up and adjust it. The first step is to refer back to the rulebook and find out what restrictions are in place for your division/sport. If your gear is dual use gear (used for carry and competition) then you will want to ensure that it meets the rule restrictions. Both major practical shooting governing bodies have rules in place that do not allow me to compete with the holster method and placement that I carry with. You will want to check to see if there are any problems with your gear. Here are your considerations for gear set up broken down by holster and magazine pouch:

➢ *Holster.* You will want to place your holster on your belt in a position where you can stand with your hands relaxed at your sides and without breaking your shoulder forward, or making any unnecessary movements, move your gun hand to the handgun grip. If the holster is too far forward or backward you will have to make unnecessary movement to get your gun hand on the handgun. If this is a dual use holster, then placement will also be based on your general duty/carry setup, or maybe even concealment considerations. If your holster is adjustable for height, then you will want to place it in a spot where you do not have to move your body to the side to get your hand on the gun. Once again, with your hands relaxed at your sides, you should be able to move the gun hand straight up and onto the grip of the handgun. If you can adjust cant angle, then you will want to adjust the angle so that when you place your gun hand on the grip, it drops evenly onto the backstrap (back) of the grip. A gun that is canted too far to the rear (muzzle pointing to the rear) will force you to break your shoulder to grip the gun. A gun that is canted too far forward (muzzle pointing forward) will cause you to hit the beavertail/tang area of the gun when gripping the gun. My personal position, and one I see most commonly used by the best shooters, is one where the gun is nearly straight up and down.

➢ *Magazine Pouch(es).* Check the rulebook for your sport/division to see what is allowed with the placement of the magazine pouches. One key

257

point is that if you shoot multiple divisions, then you will have the ability to place your magazine pouches in different spots. I highly recommend setting up your different competition rigs with the magazines in the same spots. In USPSA production division, the rules state (today), that the magazines must be placed behind the point of the hip bone (In IDPA they must be behind the center line). Internationally, the same magazine placement is required. Given these rules, even though I can move the magazine pouches farther forward when I shoot in the USPSA Limited or Limited-10 classes, I won't, simply for the reason that I do not want to train with my magazines in different spots, which forces me to take time to retrain every time I switch divisions or go overseas to shoot. I can also tell you that there are no performance advantages in moving magazine pouches farther forward. Now, if you are dual using gear (carry/compete), then you will want to keep your gear exactly the same. Once again, make sure what you have falls within the rules. When you are adjusting the magazine pouch for cant (if possible and legal), I recommend adjusting the magazine pouch so that you index the base pad first when grabbing the magazine. You should be able to keep your wrist at a natural and relatively straight angle when grabbing the magazine from the pouch. My magazines are pretty much straight up and down, mainly because that allows me to grab a magazine in any of my gear, which I have set up pretty much the same way. My carry gear, IDPA gear, USPSA gear, teaching gear, etc. are all pretty much the same.

Summary. In this step we have discussed the fundamental selection of gear including your firearm, holster, magazine pouches and belt system. You should be sold on the idea that it is important to invest in the best gear you can, even if this means sacrificing in some other areas (skip that steak dinner twice).

BONUS 2
Supporting
Your Activities
Through Sponsorship

"Train hard enough, and it will come"

By: Mike Seeklander

Sponsorship 101 - Successful sponsorship is about understanding the sales and marketing processes of the companies that you wish to represent and get sponsored by. It always amazes me when I think of my own past and remember how I unknowingly violated the sponsorship rules that I write in this manual. I can only thank several legendary shooters and one in particular for teaching me the rights and wrongs of representing companies through sponsorship. I learned the hard way and got several butt chewings as a result of doing stupid stuff that did not demonstrate the professionalism I should have shown.

Here are some guidelines to finding and solidifying successful sponsorship:

> *Individual Performance.* An athlete wishing to find sponsorship should understand that while winning is not everything in terms of getting sponsorship, it certainly is important! Athletes should not place themselves in a position where they expect to find and solidify sponsorship until they have put in the time and hard work to become at least a state level champion. While some companies (like the United States Shooting Academy-USSA) do solicit and select team members that are not at that level yet, those companies have a specific purpose in doing so. In general though, athletes should practice their elevator speech and be on the look out for sponsorship, yet not expect it until they have put the time in. The best sponsorship out there is usually in conjunction with working full or part time for a company, and receiving sponsorship from that company.

> *Sales and Marketing.* One of the most misunderstood portions of getting sponsorship is a lack of understanding the sales and marketing processes most companies use. Successful sales are a result of a strong sales team, and are predicated by successfully marketing. A sponsored shooter is an extension of the company's marketing and compliments the sales team of a company. If you look at the way I manage the team at USSA (U.S. Shooting Academy's shooting team), you will see that I don't refer to the team as a

"shooting" team when recruiting, I solicit applications for "marketing team" USSA. It is very important to understand that when a company pays you to use their product and represent it, you are contracted to do just that. Unfortunately, there are way too many shooters out there that look at sponsorship as "getting something for free". This is absolutely wrong, and I can tell you definitively, nothing is free. I learned this lesson the hard way and I am very grateful for a national champion level shooter who taught me that lesson. Some things you can expect a company to ask for or expect you to do for them:

- o *Collect Leads.* Leads are simply potential customers for the business. Some businesses have a sales team who will follow up with those leads by calling them, and others will simply market their products to those potential customers by sending them a marketing package or brochure of some sort. As an ambassador of the company, your job is to speak to everyone you can about the company and their products or services, and when you meet someone who may be interested, collect their information so your company can follow up. It is amazing how many people are out there that don't understand that they will get better sponsorship and build life long relationships with companies if they simply work a bit while they are at shooting matches.

- o *Evangelize the Company.* Okay, maybe I am sounding strong here, but if you don't really believe in their products and services, you should not be sporting their company logo. Good sponsorship is really hard to find these days, and when you get sponsored by a good company it is up to you to build that relationship by doing anything

261

you can to spread the word about that company. Let everyone know how good the company is, and how good their products are. Once again, if you don't believe this, then get out of the sponsorship deal. How much is some small sponsorship worth if you don't believe in the product? At best, you are going to dislike what you have to use, and at worst you will default to using something else which will look dishonorable to the company. If you don't happen to like some certain design feature then tell the company how they can improve the product. Good companies will listen, and may make an attempt to change things. If not, hang in there, as it is not that easy to just stop and change the production of a certain product. If a company will not listen to any of your suggestions, once again, why are you working for them?

o **Communicate Product Knowledge**. If you represent a company, you should know everything about it! One of my first big sponsors was Phil Strader and his company *Shooters Paradise*, in Virginia. I knew Phil well and we had a great time shooting together, but I honestly did not know a thing about the company until later in the second year of my sponsorship. Shame on me. Even though Phil just wanted me to do well at the matches I went to and never put any tasks on my plate, I owed it to him and the business to educate myself about it so I could help promote it. When you get a sponsorship deal, or just free products, make sure you take the time to get to know the product line well.

o **Use the Product.** It seems this would go without saying, but I have seen (and done this myself in the past), people take free products and not use them. It is not uncommon to be offered free products when you get to the upper levels of shooting, and it is very important that you understand one thing: Get a definitive agreement up front when you take free stuff from someone. Let them know exactly what you plan to do with it, whether it is to use or test the product. Make sure they agree to this and find out if they want the product back if you plan not to use it. Find out if there are obligations to using the product, for example, does the company want you to use the product 100% of the time, or just while you are shooting certain matches? If you're not going to use a product, I will send it back to the company (I learned this the hard way). Some companies will get insulted when you send something back, so if there is an improvement that you would recommend, tell them. If they will work with you, then this may be a company that you might want to stick with. If not, then let them know up front the product does not meet your expectations, and that you are respectfully sending it back to them.

Athlete/Sponsorship relationship - The way you treat your sponsors and how they treat you may be a key in the future relationship with the company. Some of the following recommendations may not be mandatory, but may go a long way to building a successful relationship!

➢ ***Honest and Open communication*** - This is the biggest mistake I have made in the past. My mistake, and the problem with new shooters and some of the younger generation is that they don't always understand what they are obligated to do with products given to them. Here is how it usually goes down: A newer shooter works his way up to some decent performances or wins at some big matches. During this climb in skill and name recognition, the athlete is given some free product from Company A. The athlete, having worked his way to the top skimping on everything, obviously takes the product, without any

263

conversation about obligations. The athlete then uses a competing product, or does not use the product at all, but hey, it was free and there were no obligations right? I was once told that "nothing is free". Any company that gives you something has some expectations from it. Make sure that you get those expectations out in the open with some sort of discussion. Ask the company how and when they require that you use that product, now that they have given it to you. My suggestion is that you either use it or offer to send it back. Obviously, if the product works well and you like it, you will probably use it. In this case, let the company know when you will be using the product and when you might not use it (maybe certain divisions or matches where it won't work well). In summary, just make sure you communicate this to the company and that you both have a clear understanding.

➢ ***Get it in writing*** - If you are to represent a company and their products and services, you should have a clear understanding of what they expect you to do. Even if it is a simple email with some details on what they expect, try to get a company representative to let you know in writing the specifics of your deal. This is important when it comes to getting product or payment, if a company does not provide what they promised. An agreement in writing also lets companies know that you are a professional, and plan to abide by whatever agreement you make.

➢ ***Communicate on a schedule***. I can't imagine how displeased I would be if I sponsored someone to represent USSA and never heard from them during the shooting year. Keep in touch with your sponsors and let them know how you are doing on the circuit. I suggest something like a match report that you can submit to your sponsors after each match you shoot. The match report I suggest will report on things such as match finish, product performance, and most importantly, potential business that you may be sending their way. This may be the most important point; after all, you are trying to help them sell more of their products or services.

> **Be Loyal.** Athletes who bounce from company to company tend to develop a reputation that they probably do not deserve. Loyalty goes a long way in this world so unless you have a real good reason to switch to another company, I recommend you try to stick with who helped you out in the beginning. Companies will appreciate this very much, and when they like you, they will communicate this to other companies. Everyone in the shooting industry knows everyone else, so this may be important for your reputation.

> **Send Thanks.** A yearly card at the seasons close will go a long way in saying thank you to your sponsors. If nothing else, drop them a quick email or better yet, call them. I wish I had been better at this earlier in my career. Now I make an effort to say "thanks" to the couple companies that help me out. I can't say this enough- that getting sponsorship is a matter of developing relationships. Tell the folks who send you boxes of gear "thanks" every chance you get!

> **Keep your stats.** It might be a smart idea to keep track of the business that you send your sponsors as well as how you are doing in your performances. I would keep a yearly "sponsored shooter resume" that can be sent to a sponsor at their request that shows key data that might be useful to them. A yearly review might solidify future sponsorship, and if nothing else you can refer to your history when speaking with potential sponsors. If you can show them how you increased sales for other companies, you have a better chance at getting sponsorship support.

By: Mike Seeklander

Summary: **Lets summarize the Supporting Your Activities Through Sponsorship section:**

- ☐ As you get better and better, you may have opportunities to become sponsored and receive monetary or other compensation for promoting a company or its products. Key guidelines to sponsorship are:
    - o Individual skill and results are important.
    - o Sales and marketing are key parts of the company you support, and you are now part of that process.
    - o Collecting leads (potential business/customers) may be part of the requirement, so you should be prepared to meet as many people as you can and tell them about your sponsor.
    - o Evangelize the company each chance you get.
    - o Make sure you know, and can communicate about the products or consumables that the company you represent sells.
    - o Use the product!
- ☐ Keys to the sponsor/athlete relationship:
    - o Honest and open communication
    - o Key contractual obligations in writing
    - o Communicate on a schedule (regular emails and phone calls)
    - o Be loyal at all times
    - o Send thanks at the end of each shooting year
    - o Keep your stats (how well you did during the year, and who you met)

I would like to give special thanks to the following companies that have supported me along the way. I owe them a great deal and appreciate all they have done for me.

➤ The United States Shooting Academy (www.usshootingacademy.com)
  ○ The U.S. Shooting Academy (my current employer) is the premier training and membership facility in the United States. They offer the best training available from world-class trainers. In addition, USSA has a complete custom gun shop, currently staffed by Kevin Toothman (the best 1911/2011 gunsmith I have ever met).

➤ Safariland (www.safariland.com)
  ○ Safariland is the premier designer of the best holsters and firearm accessories on the planet. I have been using their products for more than 5 years, and have not found anything comparable. They offer competition, as well as self-defense products for handguns, rifles and shotguns.

By: Mike Seeklander

- ➤ Smith and Wesson Firearms (www.smith-wesson.com)
  - ○ Smith and Wesson builds the best firearms in the world. Their M&P line of handguns and rifles have been my primary competition and self defense guns for several years now, by my own choice. They have been a staple in the U.S. as one of the original companies building guns and are still building great products today.

Bonus 3
A Sampling
of Technique

"Technique that does not change, is trash"

By: Mike Seeklander

Technique – This section was taken directly from the Shooting-Performance coaching manual. This manual is deliberately light on technique, because I am a big believer that technique should constantly evolve. For this reason, I prefer to relay technique in person, or by video. I could not bring myself to publish this book without any reference to technique as I teach it, and thought this section would be useful to the newer competitors that are beginning, or searching for something to help their shooting. If you desire more on technique, as I have stated elsewhere in this book, contact me.

Firing Cycle - The firing cycle is the most important thing you can understand and apply in your training sessions. The Firing cycle is the process of firing a shot or multiple shots. This seems simple, and is in theory. Theory doesn't do much for us when we are under pressure of any kind, and mistakes in the firing cycle are the primary reason we miss shots. The firing cycle isn't much different for someone shooting a match or in combat, but I will try to point out the differences. The breakdown of the process is as follows:

➤ *Locate and stop the gun on the target.* This may be from the draw (holster) or after shooting a separate target. This is a visual and physical process. Locating the target is the process of knowing where is it (previous knowledge) or finding the target and looking at it (some stimulus like a noise indicates that the target is there). Visual attention must be specific, meaning that we must look exactly where we want to point the gun. Pointing the gun at the target is simply the process of moving the gun in a straight line as aggressively as possible to point toward it. During this process we would also be doing some things with the trigger (possibly), as well as the sights.

➤ *Prep (prepare) the trigger.* Note: Understand that this is for a shot where we have already MADE the decision to shoot. It is the physical process of placing the finger on the trigger and taking the slack out of single action triggers (the

270

slack is any movement before we approach that "wall" at the sear break or release point). Prepping a double action trigger can vary from trigger to trigger, but is generally the process of pulling the trigger enough to bring the hammer back to the point where it is very close to releasing forward again. Some double action triggers have a "wall" or stiff spot right before they release forward again, and this is where we should attempt to be with the trigger to "prep" it. The process of prepping the trigger should occur during the last 5% of the extension of the gun, or on multiple targets the trigger should be prepped as the front sight enters the target area (before the gun stops). Key Note (slapping, riding): When we prep the trigger there may or not be a measurable pause at that "wall" where we have reached the sear release point. Lighter triggers like those that are found on most competition guns would require much less attention to reaching this prepped point and pausing for any amount of measurable time (I am talking about hundredths of a second here), and often times a good shooter may appear to be slapping or pressing straight through the "wall". The pause length at the wall will increase or decrease depending on the difficulty of the shot, and what the sights are telling the shooter. The difference in slapping the trigger and riding it (maintaining contact) will be related to the person's ability to maintain alignment of the gun while doing either.

> *Verify*. The physical process of prepping the trigger must be accompanied by the visual process of verifying the sights. As talked about above, there may be a slight pause at the prepped point of the trigger to verify the sight, or correct alignment of the gun if necessary. A mental trigger should be trained and ran in practice and dry fire that forces you to verify that the sights are visually referenced and in focus (as much as needed to hit the shot), as well as aligned. This is done by prepping the trigger and consciously telling yourself to bring a

By: Mike Seeklander

focus back to the sights at that same time (pressure on the trigger finger keys this thought).

➤ *Grip and Lock, Stabilize and Press.* This is the physical action of gripping the gun with the final firing pressure, locking the wrist and elbow tendons, and stabilizing the gun through the final process of pressing the trigger. NOT MOVING THE GUN IS THE GOAL. This process makes the gun go bang....

➤ *Follow Through, Reset and Prep.* This is the process of following the sights during recoil, identifying exactly where the front sight was during the initial point of recoil (this tells us where we hit the target, and is known as calling the shot). When the recoil occurs, we are deciding if we hit or not based on the sight picture (and for you combative guys, the response of the threat). Reset of the trigger occurs by getting the trigger finger off of the trigger and forward to the reset point as fast as possible, and is the critical part of the process. It can best be described as "getting off the trigger quickly, and back on to re-prep the trigger as fast as possible. Some shooters ride the trigger, and some come all of the way off of it, either of which is acceptable as long as they do the important thing, which is allowing the trigger to reset. Failure to get "off the trigger" may result in having what is called trigger freeze, which is when the shooter can't shoot an additional shot due to the fact they have not reset the trigger.

➤ *Decide, and Repeat.* We should have called the shot as well as assessed the hit via the sights (competitive shooters) or the target/threat response (combative and competitive shooters). The decision is ours to take another shot or not, as the gun should have been returned to target, the trigger should be prepped, and the sights verified...just waiting for the press if applicable.

The entire process from one step to another must be repeated for each shot. Locate and stop the gun>prep the trigger while verifying while gripping and locking>stabilize and press>follow through while resetting and prepping>decide and repeat (if necessary).

TRIGGER MANAGEMENT (how to pull it correctly) -

Trigger finger placement - The trigger finger placement is less critical than most people think. If you have normal length fingers, place the finger on the trigger somewhere around the first pad of the finger. The pad should contact the front of the trigger, and it is important that the finger is not applying pressure to one side or the other. This may cause the shooter to push or pull the gun to the right or left, thus moving the gun off alignment. Placement should allow for trigger pressure to be straight to the rear on the front most point of the trigger.

Trigger finger movement - Movement of the trigger finger is described under the firing cycle, and can be summarized as: "prep, press, reset-prep, press. To allow the shooter to pull the trigger straight to the rear, the trigger finger should be isolated so that the only portion of the finger moving is the end of the finger from the second joint to the tip. The meatier big portion of the finger is isolated and does not move when the trigger is pulled, this will ensure that the shooter does not press on the side of the gun and move it off target. The real secret is: isolating and moving ONLY the trigger, forward of the second joint without moving anything else. Common mistakes include unlocking the wrist and moving the gun out of alignment and milking (gripping) the gun as the trigger is being pulled (instead of isolating the trigger finger, all of the gripping fingers squeeze).

By: Mike Seeklander

Sight Management -

Equal height and light - Most people get it when it comes to aligning the sights. We need to have the ability to center the front within the rear, and place the front on the target where we want to hit it. Some common mistakes: Using the whole front sight instead of the top edge and corners when making a precise shot. Some people also make the mistake of using the dot on the front sight, which is meant for quick reference, not precise aiming. Worrying too much about perfect alignment at handgun range (0-15 yards). After 15 yards, or on a hard shot we need to start working a bit, but before that, if the front sight is somewhere in the notch, the bullet will hit the target. Try this on the range! Shifting focus from the front sight to the target too soon. This keeps us from watching the front sight during recoil, and also does not allow us to call the shot, since most of the time we are focused on the target (worrying about our hit) and don't see the sight lift.

Grip Management (recoil control) -

General - Gripping the gun is one of the most critical processes in shooting a handgun, and this is primarily because controlling the recoil is so important to us because we want to fire fast repeat shots. At USSA we teach that the mechanics of the grip need to offer maximum leverage and friction benefits against the handgun. Handguns recoil travels in one key direction, and therefore there are also key areas of the handgun grip that are important when we look at where we want to apply pressure to control recoil. Lets break the grip down:

Leverage - Applying leverage against the gun is incredibly important when trying to control recoil. The axis of recoil for a handgun travels rearward on a line equal to the height of the barrel, and because the grip of a handgun extends down, the farther down the grip we move our hand, the less we can control recoil. Both strong and support hands must be placed as high on the grip of the handgun as possible. We increase our recoil control by increasing our leverage on the gun.

Friction - This is a key area that some shooters make mistakes on when gripping a handgun in what some describe as a "thumb over thumb" grip. The grip panels on a handgun usually have some sort of checkering or aggressive surface that is designed to create friction between our hands and the grip. This friction allows us to control the handgun better and limit its movement upward and rearward during recoil. Keys to using these friction areas are a matter of placing our hands on the grip so we maximize our skin contact with the grip panels. When gripping with the strong hand, we must keep our strong hand thumb high (called flagging it) allowing our support hand to make as much contact with the grip panel as possible.

Pressure Areas - Placing pressure on the handgun grip is the key to controlling recoil, but it is important to understand where pressure is important, and where it is not. The key area is: the back of the gun (back strap). Most shooters spend a ton of working at griping and applying pressure to the wrong areas of the gun. The simple fact is that the gun recoils along the axis of the bore to the rear, and most of the recoil force is transmitted to the rear. Building a solid foundation against the rear of the grip is the best way to control recoil without having to over grip the gun. How much pressure should we grip the gun with? Enough to control recoil! This seems simple, but the best way to ensure you are gripping the gun tight enough is to watch the sights. When gripping correctly, the gun will recoil and snap back to alignment. Over gripping the gun will cause fatigue, and a possible shaking, and limited motion of the trigger finger. Take your strong handgrip, grip an unloaded handgun with your finger on the trigger. Increase the pressure until you lose the ability to move your trigger finger quickly and without tension, and then back off the pressure again until you can move your trigger finger freely. That is about enough pressure to grip the gun properly. The support hand should be the gripping hand that applies the most pressure. I won't get into the ratio (like 60/40) because I have never found it to be relevant. I grip the gun relatively hard with both hands

275

when at full extension and shooting. The true secret is to focus on hand placement, vs. grip pressure.

Draw Processes -

Concealment - If you wear a handgun concealed, the first consideration is getting the garment out of the way. I do not believe in the finesse methods of sweeping a t-shirt or jacket out of the way, and prefer to aggressively sweep the jacket with four fingers, or using the thumb to sweep the t-shirt up and out of the way when concealing the gun with that method.

Index points - There are points that I call index points that will allow you to grip the gun consistently, which is ultimately the goal.

- ➤ *Point 1.*   High chest area just above the solar plexus. Support hand indexes the low chest area, and does so at the same time that the strong hand indexes point two (2). The support hand should move at the same speed as the strong hand when initiating the draw process.
- ➤ *Point 2.*   Coming in from a rearward angle, from behind the gun (standing looking forward). Strong hand indexes behind the tang of the grip slightly behind the top portion of the tang. I index the gun from the rear and slide it up so that it is high on the backstrap of the gun. This ensures that my strong hand slides into the highest possible position on the grip.
- ➤ *Point 3.*   Support hand index finger at about the second joint. The support hand indexes the trigger guard and then rolls onto the strong hand where I begin to form my grip.

Move fast, shoot in control - This is a term we use to get people to do the physical movements of the draw, or other manipulations as fast as they can successfully perform the move, yet take the time to perform the firing cycle (shoot) in control.

We want to gain time in those areas! When reaching for the gun, or presenting it to the target, do it FAST!

Straight Lining - This is a term Phil Strader uses when he describes most movements in practical shooting, and it definitely applies to the draw. Basically, when the gun leaves the holster, no matter what type or where it is placed, getting the gun to point at the target is a movement that should be as straight as possible. We don't want to waste time dipping the gun low (scooping), or high (fishing). The guns muzzle should point toward the target as soon as possible, and then the gun should be presented toward the target in a straight line. This differs slightly when doing a draw at close quarters, or one used mainly for combative purposes, as we tend to keep the gun closer to the body when doing these types of draws. A draw done for combative purposes is a slightly different subject.

Reloading the Gun -

Orientation and Position - Magazine orientation and position is important. Magazines should be in the pouches so that the bullet tip (front) points forward. If you have the ability, try to set up the magazine pouches so that you can bring your support hand straight to the magazine without breaking the angle of your wrist. This may not always be possible when complying with the rules of a certain division, or when you are using one set up that you might be issued.

Index Points - Just as with the draw process or any other process, there are key points called index points that allow a shooter to grab the magazine the same way each time. This helps ensure that the reload is consistent, which to me is as important as speed, as long as the reloads are relatively fast. Index Points-

> *Point one.* Palm of the support hand on the front edge of the base pad. The
> support hand should index the magazine with the palm of the hand indexing

277

the base pad of the magazine on the front edge. This guides the rest of the hand into position and ensures that the front edge of the base pad is in solid contact with the palm, which is how the magazine will be pushed into the gun.

➢ *Point two.* Support hand index finger along the front edge of the magazine, with the tip of the finger on/or near the bullet of the first round. The actual position of the index finger will depend on the length of the magazine and the length of the shooters finger.

Types - The different types of reloads all have pretty much the same mechanics, so I won't break each down. Basically, IDPA style reloads are supposed to be more "tactical" in nature, and usually force you to retain any unused ammunition. Whether or not this is actually more "tactical" is debated in some circles, but I will break the loads down within two categories (1) Saved Magazine, and (2) Unsaved Magazine.

Saved Magazine Loads -

Reload with Retention-

➢ We release the magazine and save it by stowing it in a pocket, beltline, or elsewhere that will practically hold the magazine for future use.

➢ Index the new magazine by moving the support hand in a straight line to the new magazine and grab it utilizing the index points described above.

Tactical Reload (also called magazine exchange in some circles)-

➢ We go for the new magazine first in this reload (differing from the reload with retention where we stow the old first), indexing it as stated above. As we bring the magazine toward the gun, we slip it between our index and second finger.

- Using our index finger, we release the old magazine and pull it out.

- Rotating our hand, we then rotate and insert the new magazine, tapping it into the weapon with our palm (where it should be indexed).

- The old magazine is then stowed in a pocket, beltline, or elsewhere that will practically hold the magazine for future use.

Unsaved Magazine Loads -

Speed Reload (the primary reload used in USPSA)-

- This load is done while there is still a round (or more) in the chamber. It is (and should) be done when moving, if possible.

- Let the old magazine drop by hitting the release, while moving the support hand to the new magazine, indexing as described above.

- Orient the gun so the magazine well is pointed toward the magazine pouch on the belt. This will help when inserting the magazine because the magazine well will line up with the new magazine.

- Insert and Re-grip. Re-grip the gun by inserting the magazine firmly with the palm of the hand, and then moving the support hand upward until the index finger knuckle hits index point 3 as described under the draw section.

- Key Point: Re-Prep the trigger and take the time to see the sights if another shot is necessary. The shot right before the load, and the one after it are usually the ones that turn out to be misses.

Emergency Reload (done more when competing in IDPA, or in the USPSA single stack Division)-

- The steps under the speed reload all apply.

279

➤ During the Insert and Re-grip, the support hand thumb activates the slide release as it is re-gripping the gun. Some believe (boldly) that the slide release (called the slide lock by some) should be avoided since it will be hard to use during stress. This is only true with guns that have flat or smooth levers, and should be tested under stress. There is a slight speed advantage when using the release (vs. slingshoting or overhanding the slide with brute force), and any advantage in competition is advantageous. Test both methods, and pick one that works consistently.

Other Tips - Speed is key, but consistency is king. Fast reloads certainly help, but missed and dropped reloads cost huge amounts of time, and usually cause a shooter to make a shooting mistake (since they are trying to catch up for the time they know they lost). Work on speed, but dedicate yourself to consistency when it comes to performing reloads. Fast - Slow - Fast: this is the way we describe the reload. Fast movement (as fast as possible) to the new magazine while releasing the old one, as well as when bringing it to the magazine well. Slow describes the speed the magazine is inserted into the magazine well (at least initially). This ensures that we get the new magazine started into the magazine well properly. The second fast describes the rest of the movement, the last half of the magazine insertion, as well as the re-gripping and extension of the weapon. We want to get back on target as quickly as possible.

Magazine Grip - Don't release the grip of the new magazine until you ensure that it is started correctly into the magazine well. "Throwing" the magazine into the magazine well is one of the most common reasons that shooters miss their reloads. It is very important to maintain a good grip on the new magazine until it is partially inserted and moving into the magazine well.

Movement/Shooting On The Move -

General - Developing the ability to move through a stage in practical shooting is truly one of the things that allow certain shooters to dominate in the sport. Some examples:

1. TGO-Rob Leatham: Rob is the master of movement when it comes to finding areas in a stage that he can move through rather than stand still. His "small" continual movements keep him in position to be shooting sooner than most shooters, and he often equalizes the faster sprinters by moving through areas and positioning himself better than anyone else. I have spent hours watching his movement on video, and have noticed that he is always moving. When most people look at a shooter, they notice fast aggressive movements, but rarely see the subtle movements that someone like Rob uses to save time. Those movements include slowing through a position while shooting, yet never stopping, as well as exiting a position by shifting body weight and taking subtle steps out of a position. Broken down in a purely time equation, I would guess there are several tenths of a second to gain on both ends of a position, the entry and the exit. Rather than just standing, and then trying to aggressively move, Rob will finish his last several shots and will be leaning and moving out of position while he is still shooting. Others shooters will finish shooting and then move, losing precious time.

2. Eric Grauffel (French World Champion): Eric is arguably the most talented shooter on the planet when it comes to executing correct movement on a stage. When I first began to analyze Eric and how he moves, I did it by watching his DVD over and over. I was amazed by how Eric almost never stops on a stage (hmm are we seeing a trend here, Rob and Eric both

By: Mike Seeklander

arguably the best overall competitors on the planet never stop moving on most stages). Eric practices shooting on the move at distances where most shooters would not even consider trying to hit a target while on the move. Eric uses his athletic style combined with absolute attention to the sights or dot to hit shots at these distances. I had the pleasure of training with Eric and getting some of his movement skills broken down.

How to - There are really only a certain number of ways we can move on a stage, and I will try to simplify and provide tips and thoughts for each, shooting while walking/running (shooting on the move)-

> *Forward.* Roll the feet from heel to toe. Keep the feet narrow. Knees must be bent to cushion out upper body movement. Steps must be short (and quick). Timing is not possible; try to pay continual attention to the sights and their reference to the target, pressing the trigger when they are stable. Following through the shot, and watching where the sights were when the gun went bang is the critical factor.

> *Backward.* Roll the feet from toe to heel. When stepping to the rear, push the foot to the rear while "dragging" the toe lightly across the ground, "feeling" what the foot will travel over. Once again, keep the steps short, and the gait (width of the feet) narrow. The funny thing is we are usually more stable when moving to the rear.

> *Angles.* Nothing changes with most angles except that the upper body pivots like a tank turret toward the targets. Beyond about 45 degrees from the front, the toe of the foot in the direction of the target should point roughly toward the target. This will pivot the hips enough so that we can keep the muzzle on target.

> *Sideways.* Usually we move sideways at slower speeds and aren't really moving very fast. This movement allows us to gain a few steps over our competitors (if we get physically farther ahead on the course, we theoretically gain 1-2 tenths of a second per step. Movement should be by rolling from the outer edge of the foot to the inner edge very much like movement forward and backward. Crossing the feet is a must, even though the "tactical" guys will rant that we may trip when moving like this (how do professional sports players ever stay on their feet?).

<u>Pivots, Gun side (pivoting on the foot where the gun is)</u> - The head HAS to move first, and this critical point will cause the rest of our body to follow. While the head moves, the upper body including the shoulders should begin to pivot around. During this time, we are gripping the gun and also starting to pivot our gun side foot (on the ball of the foot) around. The direction would be clockwise for a right-handed shooter, and the opposite for a lefty. This is the pivot I feel is the most consistent and easiest to do.

<u>Pivots, Non-gun side</u> - This pivot is done basically the same, but obviously we must pay attention to our gun and when we actually remove it from the holster. If we draw too quickly, we might break the safety line and get disqualified. Be careful!

<u>Pivots, Stepping</u> - The difference in a stepping pivot and a regular pivot is that a stepping pivot is initiated by stepping (to the front or rear, usually the rear). The strong or support side foot will step forward or rearward directly in front of or behind the other foot. During this step the upper body will begin to pivot in the same direction while we grip our gun. The other foot simply steps into position finalizing the shooting stance.

By: Mike Seeklander

<u>Target Acquisition</u> - There is probably more time to gain in target acquisition than there is in just trying to shoot fast.   I'll keep this one simple:

How to -

 ➢ Fire the shot, calling it good or bad from the sights, the microsecond the front sight lifts. Mentally, we process this information very, very fast, and if we are satisfied, the gun moves immediately.

 ➢ Move the eyes to the next target (directly behind the gun) and more specifically to a point on the next target.

 ➢ Drive the gun toward that spot as fast and aggressively as possible.

 ➢ Stop the gun on target using an aggressive "braking" that stops the gun smoothly.

 ➢ As the gun stops, we should be prepping the trigger for the next shot. Be careful not to prep the trigger until the front sight enters the edge of the target area.

 ➢ When the gun stops and the front sight touches the area (spot) we want to hit, reference the rear sight quickly correcting any errors and pressing through the shot.

Reminder: We gain time by moving the gun aggressively between targets, and by being ready to finalize the shot when the gun gets there

Tip: Relax the body and grip a bit when swinging the gun on wide swings, this will allow us to move faster.

<u>Target Index Points</u> - Target index points are points on the target that we are going to aim at. Top practical shooters know that it is important that they aim at a specific spot on the target, and not just the entire aiming area. The key to finding target index points is to look at the available area left of the target in the highest scoring zone, if there is hard cover or a no shoot covering portions of it. It is important to find a key spot to look at with the vision (as specific area as possible) when acquiring and engaging the target. This is especially important to know when engaging the following types of targets:

> **_Hard Cover_** - Targets with hard cover on them cause us to aim at index points on the target that are different than normal. When shooting at normal targets, we can simply aim at the center point of the A zone or 0 zone (IDPA target), or the center of the steel. When hard cover is used to eliminate portions of the target, we should find an index point on the target that is nearest to the highest value aiming area that will still allow us to keep the shots out of the hardcover.

> **_No Shoots_** - When course designers use no-shoots to obscure targets, we must go through the same process as above. Keep in mind that no-shoot targets may cause us to lose even more points than if we shot through the hard cover and scored a miss.

> **_Obscured Targets_**. These targets may be wide open, but have been obscured by obstacles on the range, possibly because of the position we have decided to shoot the target. These targets should be dealt with the same way as targets with hard cover painted on them.

Principles of all activator type targets –

> They are designed to distract the shooter, don't let them.
> There is rarely a performance advantage to trying something tricky at the C-D level. Shoot them like any other target (front sight on brown, press the trigger).
> They NEVER move as fast as they look (don't let them intimidate you).
> Other shooters may make engaging the targets look like things are happening a lot faster that you think, remember the golden rule that everything is

285

slower when you are behind the gun, do not let another shooters pace on an activator intimidate you.

➢ At the C-D level, if at all possible activate targets first then return when they have slowed or are stationary (this is the easy way, but rarely will stages allow this to be done).

➢ Scout the stage. The only way to really learn something about a stage and its movers is to watch them several times. It is not possible to see what you need to see in a short five minute walk-through. Take the time and make the effort of scouting all stages with moving targets. Take notes!

➢ Most importantly, when possible ALWAYS BE DOING SOMETHING! This is where time is lost or gained. Find something to do (reload, shoot, move) while moving through a stage. This is very important when engaging a moving target because there is usually some activation time.

➢ Reaction time: Know it! Typically auditory reaction time is about .18 to .23. Visual reaction time is usually slower if we have to decide on something (called the decision reaction time vs. straight reaction time). This is why we see people shoot a miss or do something that they recognize immediately, but pause slightly because they haven't primed their brain with reactive options.

<u>Swingers</u> –

➢ *Speed*

    o How fast does it appear after being activated, can anything else be done while waiting?

    o How fast does it move? (if you miss the walk through, look at where the weight is placed on the swinger arm, the closer to the pivot point, the faster the swinger moves back and forth.

- How fast does it return to the engagement point (the far path of the swing where the swinger pauses slightly, usually the best spot to shoot it)

➢ *Timing*
- How much time is there after the activator is hit to do something?
- Stopwatch!
- Find the sweet spot (the spot where the target stops and pauses) This spot is the place we will shoot the target. If you don't get to watch the swinger, find the position where other shooters have engaged it (look for the brass!) and then look for the impact area in the berm/ground. This will tell you exactly where to index your gun to wait and ambush the target.

➢ *Techniques for shooting*
- *Tracking*
  - Only on very close or very slow targets
  - The gun moves with the swinger (slightly)
- *Ambush*
  - This method is where we have to know the sweet spot of the target, where does it stop at full swing and pause...that is where we press the trigger (usually can get both shots, but sometimes we must wait for the target to return, if so is there anything else we can be doing?). Here is how is would be broken down:
    - Just prior to the target entering the ambush point we have prepped and begin to press the trigger.

287

By: Mike Seeklander

- Press the trigger with an keen awareness of the front sight recoiling off brown (if we don't see that we may have missed!).
- The second shot can go off as the target begins to exit the point again, but be careful to ensure that the front sight lifts from the target, not after it left (when in doubt shoot at the target when it returns...if the hit factor warrants it)
- Remember that the shot may be hard to call, since bobbers disappear below the gun (out of the vision line).

Sliders –

➢ *Speed*
   o How fast does the target move? This will determine if we have to lead the target.
   o How far away will we shoot it? Once again target lead.
   o How much exposure does it have (how long does the shooter see the target before it disappears)
   o Does it disappear? If not, can we simply shoot it at the end of its movement?

➢ *Timing*
   o Are there more than one, if so we must time our shooting to engage the one that disappears first, or possibly the one we can see first.

➢ *Techniques for shooting*
   o Gun movement. Sliders are nothing more than moving targets similar to what we shoot at matches like Bianchi. This is the one time in our shooting that we MUST keep the gun moving to some extent.

- o Target lead will be based on the speed the target moves, and the distance away the target is (bullet speed is also a consideration, but will rarely come into play in USPSA/IPSC distances)
  - ▪ For even the fastest targets, shooters will rarely have to lead any farther than the A/C line. Remember the key is to keep the gun moving (which is VERY hard for most shooters since we always stop the gun when shooting)
  - ▪ A good aiming point is to lead the target and place the front sight just inside the A/C line, keep the gun moving and press the trigger. Remember to be careful not to track the target into a no-shoot if one is there.

Bobbers –

- ➢ *Speed*
  - o What can we get done after activating them? Typically, bobbers are slow to activate.
- ➢ *Timing*
  - o Timing is everything with bobbers. We need to know the amount of time that elapses between the bobber being in full view, disappearing, and returning to full view.
- ➢ *Techniques for shooting*
  - o Tracking-Typically we wont be able to track bobbers, most of the time they will be behind metal targets and sometimes behind no-shoots.
  - o Ambush-Bobbers have a natural pause at or near their high point very similar to swingers, this is typically where we want to be shooting at the target just like swingers as follows:

289

- Just prior to the target entering the ambush point we have prepped and begin to press the trigger.
- Press the trigger with a keen awareness of the front sight recoiling off brown (if you don't see that you may have missed.).
- The second shot can go off as the target begins to exit the point again, but be careful to ensure that the front sight lifts from the target, not after it left (when in doubt shoot at the target when it returns...if the hit factor warrants it)
- Remember that the shot may be hard to call, since bobbers disappear below the gun (out of the vision line).

Clam Shells -

➢ *Speed*

  o The speed of these targets is everything since you MUST know if you can engage it with two reasonable hits before the no-shoot target blocks the primary target.

  o Is there target area to shoot at after the clamshell has fully activated? If so, we always have a back up plan to get our hits. If not, then we need to grip it and rip it if the points are worth it.

  o Caution: In the case of completely disappearing targets, there are some clamshells that are not worth engaging for a C-D shooter. You need to know your skills and make that decision. Sometimes just leaving it and flowing to other targets will be the best solution. Remember, if you are behind the timing, you will engage a no-shoot, and lose even more points on the stage.

➢ *Timing*

  o Usually clamshells aren't timed, as they only activate once.

> *Techniques for shooting*

　　o　Remember, they are not usually as quick as they appear.

　　o　Get the gun on target first, if the clamshell is activated by a door or whatever, activate it and aggressively drive the gun to the target, so you can get the shots off as soon as you have an aiming area.

Drop-Turners -

> *Speed*

　　o　Drop-turners can appear AND disappear quickly. Their speed will usually dictate whether to fire two rounds or one per facing (if it's a double facing target)

> *Timing*

　　o　Typically "DT" targets attached to a popper take a bit of time to activate, so there may be other things the shooter can do after activation. Exceptions to this rule can be "DT" targets that move after opening a door/window or pulling an activation rope.

> *Techniques for shooting*

　　o　Most shooters feel mentally trapped into shooting "DT" targets when they are fully faced. For very fast targets, this is usually too late. Acceptable shots can be taken well before a full-faced target is available (start prepping and pulling the trigger at 50-75% faced, the A hit will still be there, just slightly oblong). This usually allows more time for multiple shots.

Stage Breakdown – Planning to shoot a stage is often a critical part of performing well in a match. Below you will find a flow chart that outlines how I go about breaking down a stage and planning to shoot it, and the following are some general details and terms you need to know:

> **Stage Markers** – Stage markers are spots on the stage that I use to help me align the gun faster on the first target in a shooting array. When you walk through a stage you will find that as you enter shooting positions with walls or other vision barriers blocking your view, the first target you will see as you actually step into the location where you will shoot from will appear in a specific location in your visual field (height). The sooner you can bring the gun to bear on this target, the faster you can shoot it. For this reason, when moving into the shooting location, if there is a spot on the wall or vision barrier that I can align the gun with, I know when that target comes into view that the gun will pointed toward the target area, at generally the right height. When entering a shooting position, I extend the gun before I get stopped, and because of this all I have left to do is find the target with my eyes, do some quick centering of the gun on the aiming point, and begin firing. Conversely a shooter with less experience might have to extend their gun, find the target, and then start their centering process where I already have all that done, giving me significant time advantages.

> **Stop Markers** – Similar to stage markers, stop markers are spots on the ground that help me make sure that I stop in the exact spot I need to in order to see, and shoot at the targets in that particular array at that location. If I fail to find and step on a specific stop marker, I risk having to adjust my feet to shoot a target in an array where there are multiple targets with a big swing involved. In the below stage, see if you can find some locations where there might be stage and stop markers you could use to better shoot the stage.

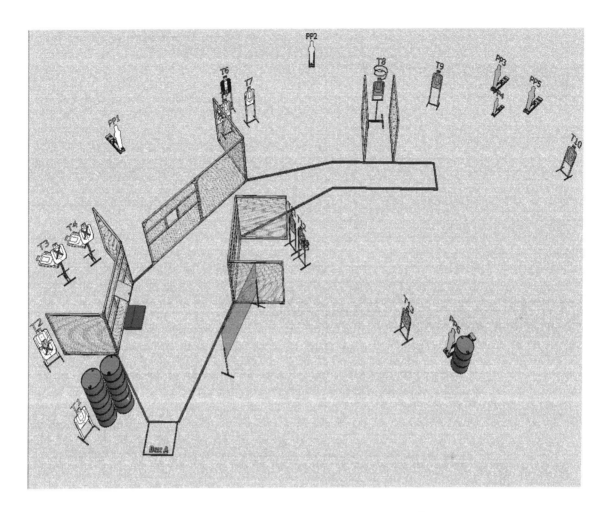

(Graphic credit Tim Egan and stage designed by Nate Martin)

> ➢ *General Stage Breakdown Tips* – The following are some things that you
>   will want to pay attention to in your stage breakdown/planning process:
>
>   o *Stay away from new things*! Stick to skills you know you have and
>   can perform on demand under stress. The only time you might want
>   to stick your neck out like that is when a title is on the line and you
>   desire to "go for it".
>
>   o *Plan reloads with some margin of error*. I have seen really good
>   shooters trash stages because they planned no reload and decided to
>   shoot to empty and had a malfunction or miss on the stage that

293

messed up their plan. The time they spent fixing the problem, and then trying to finish the stage cost them much more time than just doing a reload in a logical pause area.

o **Be careful watching shooters before you**. Good shooters make hard stuff look easy. Bad shooters make easy stuff look hard. Either way, those images can affect your self-image and hurt your performance on the stage. I strongly recommend that you do NOT look at the shooters before you when you are about to shoot. Spend that time facing away and visualizing instead.

o **Know the shooting order**. This seems so simple, but I have seen (and experienced this myself) many shooters perform poorly on a stage because they did not pay attention to the shooting order and got caught by surprise. Make sure you are prepared to shoot well before your turn.

o **Focus on the match**. If you shoot matches for social reasons, that is cool with me, but I doubt you would be reading this book if you did not have a strong desire to win. Focus on the shooting rather than socializing at matches, within reason. Obviously if you are sponsored by a company, that company will want you speaking to other shooters about their product or services, but keep these conversations to a minimum until after you have finished the stage.

o **Maintain your gear**. As described earlier in this book, I "work" matches, rather than shoot them. This means that I am constantly "working" to prepare my gear and myself for the next stage, or document the results of the last one. Check your gun and gear regularly during a match. Keep your glasses clean, magazines clean and prepared, etc.

<u>Stage Breakdown Flowchart</u> – This has been requested by several people, and may be of use to the new shooter. This flowchart will show you the process I go through to break down and stage in my planning process:

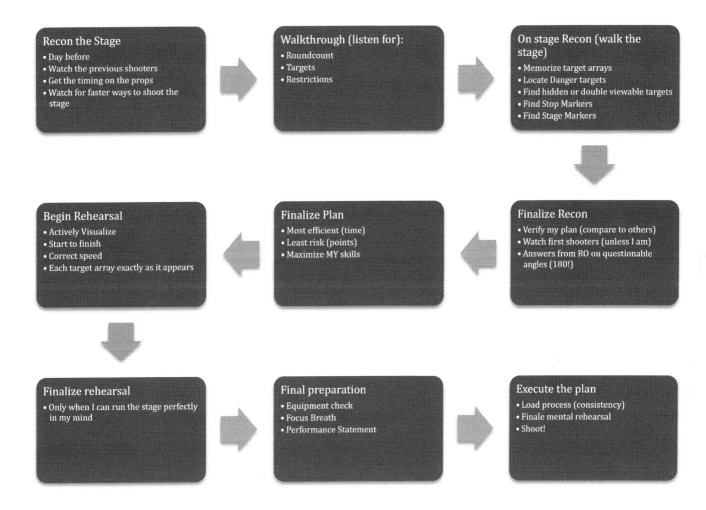

Recon the Stage
- Day before
- Watch the previous shooters
- Get the timing on the props
- Watch for faster ways to shoot the stage

Walkthrough (listen for):
- Roundcount
- Targets
- Restrictions

On stage Recon (walk the stage)
- Memorize target arrays
- Locate Danger targets
- Find hidden or double viewable targets
- Find Stop Markers
- Find Stage Markers

Begin Rehearsal
- Actively Visualize
- Start to finish
- Correct speed
- Each target array exactly as it appears

Finalize Plan
- Most efficient (time)
- Least risk (points)
- Maximize MY skills

Finalize Recon
- Verify my plan (compare to others)
- Watch first shooters (unless I am)
- Answers from RO on questionable angles (180!)

Finalize rehearsal
- Only when I can run the stage perfectly in my mind

Final preparation
- Equipment check
- Focus Breath
- Performance Statement

Execute the plan
- Load process (consistency)
- Finale mental rehearsal
- Shoot!

295

Summary:

That's the program! You have finished the book, and hopefully are ready to begin to plan your shooting year, and start training. You have all of the pieces of the puzzle; it is now up to you to put them together. Remember that action and intent are two different things, and without acting on the information that I have given you, nothing will happen. You can take bits and pieces and use them to your success, but I highly recommend you use all of the program that I have provided, as the sum of the total does not compare to the synergistic effect you will get if all are done together. I wish you much success and remember, that success favors the prepared.

Works Cited

Basham, Lanny. <u>With Winning in Mind</u>. Wilsonville: BookPartners, Inc. , n.d.

Colvin, Geoffrey. <u>Talent is Overrated</u> . New York: Penguin Group, 2008.

Coyle, Daniel. <u>The Talent Code</u>. New York: Bantam Dell, 2009.

Dintiman, George. <u>Sports Speed</u>. Champaign: Human Kinetics, 2003.

Dr. Wayne F. Martin, O.D. <u>An Insight To Sports</u>. Mill Creek: Sports Vision Inc., 1984.

Enos, Brian. <u>Practical Shooting, Beyond Fundamentals</u>. Clifton: Zediker Publishing, 1990.

Horton, Tony. <u>P90X</u>. 2004 йил 01-01. 2009 йил 01-01 <http://www.beachbody.com/p90x>.

Mack, Gary. <u>Mind Gym</u>. New York: McGraw-Hill, 2001.

Selk, Jason. <u>10-Minute Toughness</u>. New York: McGraw-Hill, 2004.

Verstegen, Mark. <u>Core Performance</u>. Pheonix: Rodale, Inc, 2004.

Wilson, Thomas. <u>SportsVision</u>. Champaign: Human Kinetics, 2004.

Special Thanks to the following shooters who took the time to fill out my survey:

1. **Ben Stoeger**, www.benstoeger.com
2. **Chuck Anderson** www.andersontactical.com
3. **Dave Olhasso**, www.olhasso.com
4. **Erik Lund**, www.usshootingacademy.com
5. **JJ Racaza**, website unknown
6. **Emanuel Bragg**, www.mannyusa.com
7. **Max Michel**, www.maxmichel.com
8. **Pat Doyle**, www.usshootingacademy.com
9. **Phil Strader**, www.straightersolutions.com
10. **Henning Wallgren**, www.henningshootsguns.com
11. **Bob Vogel**, www.vogelshootist.com
12. **Shannon Smith**, www.fastacademy.net
13. **Ted Puente**, www.frankgarciausa.com

By: Mike Seeklander

Recommended Reading:

Thinking Practical Shooting, by Saul Kirsch

Mind Gym, by Gary Mack with David Casstevens

Practical Shooting, Beyond Fundamentals, by Brian Enos

10-Minute Toughness, by Jason Selk

Warrior Speed, by Ted Weimann

Sports Vision, by Thomas A. Wilson and Jeff Falkel

With Winning in Mind, by Lanny Basham

Talent Is Overrated, by Geoffrey Colvin

More about Shooting-Performance, (www.shooting-performance.com):

Founded in 2007, Shooting-Performance is a coaching, consulting, and research company that specializes in performance related firearm instruction and information for use in both combative and competitive environments. Mike Seeklander, owner/founder has extensive experience in and has been a full time instructor since December of 2001. For more information, please visit www.shooting-performance.com.

Thanks for your interest in Shooting-Performance, and I know you will surpass your goals with the use of this program, the proper gear, and a lot of hard work. I know you can do it, now get to work!

Until Then, Train Hard!

Mike Seeklander

To order a copy of this book or other books and DVD's, please visit my website (www.shooting-performance.com)

By: Mike Seeklander

12790281R00172

Made in the USA
Lexington, KY
28 December 2011